SLADE MEDIA CENTER

W9-ARU-225

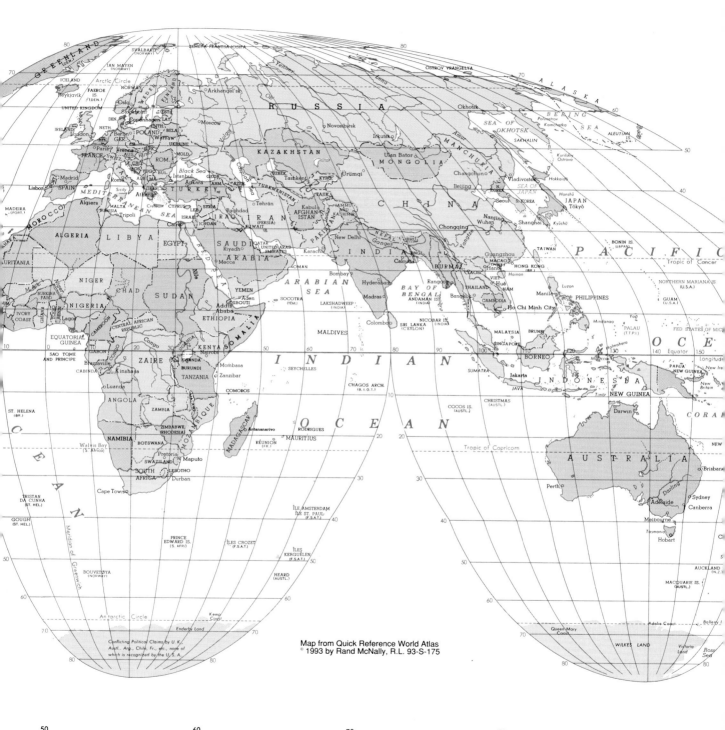

Map from Quick Reference World Atlas
© 1993 by Rand McNally, R.L. 93-S-175

Conflicting Political Claims by U.K.,
Austl., Arg., Chile, Fr., etc., none of
which is recognized by the U.S.A.

MAURITANIA	EGYPT	TANZANIA	NIGERIA	NAMIBIA	MOZAMBIQUE	ZAMBIA	ALL OTHERS 2,957	CANADA 3,850	UNITED STATES 3,787	GREENLAND	MEXICO	ALL OTHERS	BRAZIL 3,286	ARGENTINA	PERU	COLOMBIA	BOLIVIA	VENEZUELA	CHILE	ALL OTHERS	AUSTRALIA 2,966	ALL OTHERS

50   60   70   80

Map from New International Atlas
1993 by Rand McNally, R.L. 93-S-175

Enchantment of the World

PAPUA NEW GUINEA

By Mary Virginia Fox

Consultant for Papua New Guinea: Joan D. Winship, M.A., International Education and Training Consultant, Bettendorf, Iowa

Consultant for Reading: Robert L. Hillerich, Ph.D., Professor Emeritus, Bowling Green State University; Consultant, Pinellas County Schools, Florida

CHILDRENS PRESS®

CHICAGO

An artist and his work in progress

Project Editor: Mary Reidy
Design: Margrit Fiddle

Library of Congress Cataloging-in-Publication Data

Fox, Mary Virginia.
  Papua New Guinea / by Mary Virginia Fox.
    p.   cm. – (Enchantment of the world)
  Includes index.
  Summary: Discusses the geography, history, government, people, and culture of this southeast Asian country.
  ISBN 0-516-02621-6
  1. Papua New Guinea–Juvenile literature.
[1. Papua New Guinea.] I. Title. II. Series.
DU740.F64 1994   93-35493
995.3—dc20   CIP
                                               AC

Copyright © 1994 by Childrens Press®, Inc.
All rights reserved. Published simultaneously in Canada.
Printed in the United States of America.
3 4 5 6 7 8 9 10 11 R 02 01 00 99 98 97 96

Picture Acknowledgments
AP/Wide World Photos: 9, 77, 78, 85 (left)
The Bettmann Archive: 68 (right)
© **Reinhard Brucker: Field Museum, Chicago,** 45 (2 photos)
© **Cameramann International, Inc.:** Cover, Cover Inset, 12, 17, 32 (2 photos), 33 (left), 35 (right), 39, 48 (2 photos), 50 (2 photos), 51, 52, 54, 58 (bottom), 64, 71, 90, 94, 105, 108 (right), 113 (top & bottom left)
© **Joan Dunlop:** 30 (right), 33 (right), 38, 79

H. Armstrong Roberts: 75
North Wind Picture Archives: 43, 65, 68 (left)
Odyssey/Frerck/Chicago: © Wendy Stone, 14, 56, 58 (top)
Photri: 15, 28 (bottom right), 57 (left)
Reuters/Bettmann: 86 (2 photos)
Root Resources: © Byron Crader, 8 (left), 72; © Anthony Mercieca, 22 (left); © Mary & Lloyd McCarthy, 27 (right), 98
© **Bob and Ira Spring: Cover Inset** 5, 13, 16, 18 (2 photos), 28 (top & bottom left), 35 (left), 37, 40, 49, 83, 91, 100, 101 (2 photos), 102, 103 (2 photos), 104, 112
Tom Stack & Associates: © John Cancalosi, 22 (top right); © Dave Watts, 22 (bottom right); © Roy Toft, 24 (left); © Jack Reid, 26 (bottom left & right); © Larry Tackett, 34
Stock Montage: 66
Tony Stone Images: © David Austen, 4, 8 (right), 20, 108 (left), 113 (left); © Darryl Torckler, 6; © Oliver Strewe, 55
SuperStock International, Inc.: © Robin Smith, 7; © Larry Prosor, 25 (left); © David Northcott, 26 (top left); © Holton Collection, 41
© **Sam Talarico:** 30 (left), 36
UPI/Bettmann: 85 (right)
Valan: © Dr. A. Farquhar, 23 (left); © John Cancalosi, 23 (right), 24 (right), 25 (right); © Joyce Photographics, 27 (left); © Paul L. Janosi, 57 (right)
Len W. Meents: Maps on 100, 104
Courtesy Flag Research Center, Winchester, Massachusetts 01890: Flag on back cover
Cover: Terrain in the highlands in Markham Valley
Cover Inset top: Village house along the Sepik River
Cover Inset bottom: Port Moresby harbor and business district

Rouna Falls on the Laloki River near Port Moresby

TABLE OF CONTENTS

Chapter 1

INDEPENDENCE

On September 16, 1975, the territory of Papua New Guinea became an independent country. The news spread slowly from the coastal villages to the rugged highlands. Many citizens of this new self-governing republic were not sure what all the fuss was about. They had been living isolated, independent lives for hundreds of years. However, the announcement called for a celebration.

One by one, family groups began to come together. Village groups planned for dances and *sing-sings*–ceremonies involving stylized, mystical chants and music that have been performed for generations. Even rival groups put down their weapons, at least temporarily, to test the new spirit of togetherness.

The ceremonial dress of the inland people included not much more than paint, feathers, and heavy shell ornaments. It was the same dress they might have worn to celebrate a successful head-hunting raid on an enemy village years ago. Notable warriors displayed elaborate bird-of-paradise plumed headpieces attached to their hair. Bones or wooden barbs pierced their nostrils. Colored clay streaked the bodies of the men, who often have intricate patterns of elaborately scarred skin–proof that they are mature members of their group.

Opposite page: Ceremonial dress usually includes designs made with paint, feathers, and shell ornaments.

The contrast in cultures can be seen in the young village dancers in ceremonial dress (left) and a young urban family (right).

Even the women, who stayed on the sidelines for some of the more active weapon-wielding dances, were painted in vivid patterns. Cowrie shells hung from the necks of those wealthy enough to display their treasures.

In rejoicing, shouted chants were accompanied by banging hollow tubes together; water-filled bamboo poles shushed to rhythms; leather-covered drums were beaten; chips of wood attached to woven cords were whirled, making screeching noises above the rest of the sounds. It was as if nothing had changed for these inland people hidden away from the rest of the world, which was almost the truth.

On the coast in the capital city of Port Moresby, a different celebration took place. Here there had been contact with outsiders for a hundred years or more. A veneer of Western culture had been spread to this area, which is more accessible to outside trade.

Prime Minister Michael Somare

The new prime minister, Michael Somare, was dressed in a business suit. To prove that Somare would represent all areas of his country, a few chiefs of the highland clans had been brought to the city for the official celebration of raising the flag of the new nation. The splendid red-and-black banner is marked with a golden bird of paradise to the right, and five white stars form the Southern Cross constellation in the lower left field of the flag to identify Papua New Guinea's place under the heavens.

The highlanders were quick to understand that they had a new totem, a new fetish to "worship," but other modern wonders were frightening. An electric light looked like a sun in a bottle. Some highlanders had never seen cars, although airplanes—monstrous birds, they called them—had sometimes flown over their villages.

At one point a news video was shown. Even brave jungle warriors hid their faces from such magic. How could people appear on a flat screen bigger than life and then disappear without a trace? Yet the highlanders were surprised at the seeming poverty of the coastal people because none wore necklaces of shells or mother-of-pearl plates. These were signs of wealth and status in the world the highlanders knew.

When the highlanders returned home, few of their families would believe their tales. This was still a country familiar with its own past, not quite ready for the technology of the present.

THE LAND

Papua New Guinea includes part of the island of New Guinea. New Guinea is bigger than any other noncontinental island in the world except Greenland. Besides the eastern portion of New Guinea, Papua New Guinea also includes many islands to the north, the east, and the south. Papua New Guinea stretches 1,294 miles (2,082 kilometers) from north-northeast to south-southwest and 718 miles (1,155 kilometers) from north-northwest to south-southeast. The country lies between the equator and 12 degrees south latitude. Its nearest neighbors are Australia to the south, the Federated States of Micronesia to the north, and the Solomon Islands to the east. Its only shared land border is with Indonesia to the west.

Papua New Guinea and its many offshore islands are part of a great arc of mountains that extends through Asia and Indonesia and out into the Pacific Ocean.

Situated between Asia and Australia, Papua New Guinea offers interesting comparisons between the two continents. Many believe that once, many years ago, the island of New Guinea was connected to these landmasses. In time the land to the west sank, and great pressure within the earth's crust folded mountains into ridges. As the landmass of New Guinea was cut off with an ever-widening channel of water, the plants, animals, and human life were isolated and forced to adapt to select environments.

In spite of its location close to the equator, Papua New Guinea is a land of climate extremes–from steamy jungle to a few snow-capped mountains. The coastline is frequently bordered by impenetrable swamps, or it may rise directly to steep mountains. Vegetation is often very dense. Nearly everywhere are steep slopes, jagged ridges, and fast-flowing, often torrential, rivers that make travel difficult. Even today, the airfields that have been built are hemmed in by mountains, and there are few good harbors on the coast.

AN ISLAND DIVIDED

The island of New Guinea is politically and geographically divided. The western half is called Irian Jaya. For almost four hundred years Irian Jaya was part of the Dutch East Indies. Today it is part of the Republic of Indonesia.

The eastern half of the island is part of Papua New Guinea. It was formed by the merger of the territory of Papua, which had been under Australian rule from 1906 until independence, with the Trust Territory of New Guinea, a former German possession, which Australia took over at the beginning of World War I. The territory on this main island makes up about 85 percent of the nation's total land area.

The mountains are the major physical feature of Papua New Guinea. There is only one area on the mainland where mountains do not dominate the view. That is in the southern section where the Fly River runs.

Manam Volcano erupted in 1952.

Without the high mountain peaks, Papua New Guinea would not receive as much rain. An average of more than 60 inches (152 centimeters) of rain falls each year. At the Kikori River delta in the south the yearly rainfall exceeds 300 inches (762 centimeters), and the slopes of the main ridges facing the prevailing winds may receive up to more than 400 inches (1,016 centimeters) annually, making it possibly the wettest area on earth.

Papua New Guinea lies in the equatorial belt, where the northwest monsoons blow from December to April and the southeast trade winds and dry season occur from May to October. As the winds are forced up and over the mountains, the moisture they carry is condensed and released as rain.

The nation lies in one of the most unstable zones in the world. A ring of volcanoes is located offshore in two large arcs, one starting close to the north coast and curving up through the island of New Britain, the other starting in Bougainville and continuing south through the Solomon Islands. The Solomon Islands are a group of islands southeast of Papua New Guinea in the South Pacific Ocean.

Opposite page: Trees and grass cover the highland slopes.

Tropical rain forests in the south

THE SOUTH COAST

The Oriomo Plateau covers most of southwestern Papua New Guinea. It is only about 200 feet (61 meters) above sea level and is covered by soil washed down from the highlands. The plateau is covered with grassland and some scrub. This part of the land is stable and has not changed much in contour in several thousand years. In fact, this part of the island is an extension of the ancient Australian continental rocks that make up the bed of the shallow waters of the Torres Strait, which separates Papua New Guinea from Australia.

North of the Oriomo Plateau, the great delta plains of the Fly, Bamu, Turama, and Kikori rivers form part of one of the most extensive swamps in the world. For twenty miles (thirty-two kilometers) inland the land does not rise above sea level. From the air, mangrove forests and stands of nipa palms seem to indicate solid ground, but wherever there is a break in foliage, gray, brackish water can be seen.

A busy dock on the Fly River

Farther inland swampy grasslands, reed marshes, and lakes are part of the terrain. The grasslands are actually floating meadows of aquatic grasses that may stretch for miles in either direction. Geologists tell us that this part of New Guinea is slowly sinking, but at the same time it is gradually filling up with sediment brought down from the ranges to the north by torrential rains. Through this area runs the Fly River, the largest river in New Guinea. It is 700 miles (1,127 kilometers) long and is navigable for 500 miles (805 kilometers) in all seasons, making it one of the few inroads to the interior.

THE VICTOR EMANUEL RANGE

Inland from the south coast a band of foothills gradually rises to the Victor Emanuel Range. Over the years the land has shifted and split into jagged ridges. Remnants of old volcanoes, such as Mount Bosavi, Mount Favenc, and Mount Murray, still spike the landscape. In some areas volcanic rock gives way to layers of

Mount Wilhelm

limestone. The rock is honeycombed and has been worn away in weird shapes. Some slabs seem to stand on end. Sink holes are frequent and subterranean rivers suddenly disappear mysteriously into the earth. There are no running streams because rain water immediately sinks into the porous limestone. It is not an easy country to cross, and few have tried.

The highest peak in the territory is Mount Wilhelm at 14,793 feet (4,509 meters). Many of the ranges have peaks well over 10,000 feet (3,048 meters) in elevation. Some of the ranges are separated from each other by broad, grass-covered, highland valleys. Here the climate is moderate, and here is where some of the most densely populated areas of New Guinea are found.

THE VALLEYS

Running parallel to the Victor Emanuel Range is a great gash in the landscape. Here are the wide valleys of the Sepik, Ramu, and

A valley in the highlands

Markham rivers. In the plains the rivers lose their rushing current and deposit their load of soil. The streams separate into braided paths of water that meander through the floodplains, creating more swamps and lakes. Away from the marshes the land rises in a gradual slope to the northern mountains.

The northern chain of mountains is neither as wide nor as high as the Victor Emanuel Range. There is a big break where the Sepik and Ramu rivers enter the sea. This area is one of recent elevation–formed gradually within the last ten thousand to twenty thousand years. Beds of coral rock are found two hundred to three hundred feet (sixty-one to ninety-one meters) above sea level.

THE ISLANDS

Other islands governed by the Papua New Guinea Parliament include the Bismarck Archipelago, from the Ninigo group and the

*The southern tip of Bougainville Island (above)
and a hot spring on New Britain (right)*

Admiralty Islands north of Papua New Guinea to the string of
small land groups curving eastward to New Britain. The most
easterly of the larger islands is Bougainville, and trailing off the
southern tip of the main landmass of Papua New Guinea are the
D'Entrecasteaux Islands, Woodlark, and the Louisiade Island
groups.

New Britain, the largest of the islands, was formed at the same
time as the northern mountains of Papua New Guinea. Volcanoes
are common and some are still active. On the Willaumez
Peninsula is a vast area of geysers and hot springs. At the north
end of New Britain is the Gazelle Peninsula, the most
commercially developed area in Papua New Guinea. Simpson
Harbor, where Rabaul is located, was formed when the sea
flooded the cone of an extinct volcano.

All the other large islands in the group, from the Admiralty
Islands through New Ireland, are the tops of a submerged
mountain range running parallel to the Victor Emanuel Range.

Active volcanoes include Balbi and Bagana on Bougainville. Mount Lamington erupted in 1951, killing nearly three thousand people. In 1994 Vulcan and Tavurvur nearly destroyed Rabaul.

VEGETATION

Since New Guinea is near the equator, temperatures in the lowland areas reflect little seasonal change. Only in the higher elevations is there relief from the heat and humidity. Rarely does the temperature climb above 90 degrees Fahrenheit (32.2 degrees Celsius) or dip below 70 degrees Fahrenheit (21.1 degrees Celsius), but for those unaccustomed to the humidity it is not a pleasant climate. In contrast, at about 10,000 feet (3,048 meters) frosts are common, and on Mount Wilhelm snow occasionally falls.

The year is divided into two seasons: the "wet" season and "dry" or "not so wet" season. These seasons correspond to the period when the southeast trade winds and the northwest winds prevail. Port Moresby is an exception to this rule. Here the winds blow parallel to the coast. Between the seasons there is a calm that often is oppressive.

Broadly speaking, the vegetation of the island falls into six categories, depending on elevation. Temperatures generally fall by about three degrees Fahrenheit for each thousand feet of altitude. Each climate zone has its own type of vegetation: rain forest, mangrove swamp, savanna woodland, open grassland, oak and beach forest, and alpine moor. Each climate zone tends to have its own distinctive animal population as well. This affects how humans live, what they eat, how they hunt, and how they build their houses. Every aspect of their lives is affected by their environment.

THE RAIN FOREST

Tropical rain forests cover about 85 percent of the main island. At least two hundred different species of trees flourish in the lowland rain forest. The forest trees range from 35 feet (11 meters) to 150 feet (46 meters) in height. There are shrubs less than 20 feet (6 meters) tall with many wild seedlings, mosses, and ferns. All are laced together with many climbing plants, creepers, and thorny rattan. In places it is impossible to cut a path through the jungle, yet in other areas the tall trees completely block out sunlight so the forest floor is almost bare.

A DIFFERENT FOREST

At about 3,000 feet (914 meters) grow laurel, oak, beech, red cedar, nutmeg, local mahoganies, and the commercially important Araucaria forest of linkii and hoop pine. These tall pines are cut and placed in giant peeling machines that shave them into thin sheets used for plywood. Woody vines disappear at this altitude and are replaced by giant ferns. Areas that have been cleared for lumber are covered with tall sword grass, a type of wild cane.

UP THE MOUNTAINSIDE

At about 9,000 feet (2,743 meters) the forest changes to gnarled and crooked trees only about 30 feet (9 meters) in height, festooned with thick blankets of dripping moss. At about 11,000 feet (3,353 meters) above the misty mountain forest, where the air is drier and sunnier, evergreens have found a roothold. Above 12,000 feet (3,658 meters) the vegetation consists of Alpine grasses, yellow buttercups, and deep blue gentians.

Opposite page: A river cuts through the dense rain forest.

*Tree kangaroos (left), a bandicoot (top right), and
a ring-tailed possum (above right)*

WILDLIFE

Nearly 180 mammals living in Papua New Guinea have been
identified and described. Many are *nocturnal*, only active at night.
Large areas of the country have never been explored, so the
number of animals native to this part of the world may be much
larger.

About one-third of the mammals are *marsupials*, animals that
protect their young in the mother's pouch until they are weaned.
Australian kangaroos are the best-known variety of marsupials,
but this species comes in many sizes. Tree kangaroos, cuscuses,
and ring-tailed possums live high in the tree canopy. Cuscuses are
thought to be marsupial "monkeys." They are about the size of a

A fruit bat (left) and an echidna (right)

cat, but have long tails. They have fine, dense fur. On the ground live wallabies, bandicoots, marsupial "cats," and pouched "mice."

Papua New Guinea has many strange life-forms. An egg-laying mammal called an echidna is found here. Seventy kinds of bats make their homes in caves and trees.

Some of the most beautiful birds in the world live here. The country contains 660 known species, more than the total for all of Europe. Many sport exotic colors. Their bright plumage has two purposes. Since visibility is often limited in the forest, the birds' vivid colors serve to advertise their presence to others of their kind, making sure that mating will occur. The bright colors also act as camouflage against the colorful background of a jungle forest. The superb fruit dove, for instance, with its pattern of yellow, green, orange, purple, and black feathers, blends into the

More than 660 known species of birds, including fruit doves (left) and bower birds (right), live in Papua New Guinea.

dappled light and shade of the tree canopy. Only another dove would be able to pick out the shape of the bird when it is perched in a tree. Raggiana birds display waterfalls of orange plumes.

When Europeans saw some of these spectacular birds, they set up a trade with the inhabitants to kill the birds for their gorgeous plumage. At the beginning of the twentieth century, thousands of birds-of-paradise skins were being exported every year from New Guinea. Most turned up in fancy milliners' shops in Paris. In no time at all the birds were hunted almost to extinction. Today they are protected by law. Most of these birds live in the lowland and mid-mountain forests.

The bower bird has been studied for its elaborate mating ritual. To attract a mate the male of the species clears a large area of brush. He fences it in and decorates it with brightly colored seeds and flowers. The mating pair then performs a courtship dance.

Another unusual bird is the cassowary, a flightless bird about 3

The black-and-white banded sea snake (left) and a cassowary (right)

feet (0.9 meter) tall–larger than a domestic turkey. It was killed for food and almost wiped out by hunters. Its sharp talons are still used for decoration and also as sharp-bladed instruments. It resembles the Australian emu.

Papua New Guinea has the largest pigeon in the world and the smallest parrot. Other oddities are still being discovered.

Many varieties of snakes live in the swampland and on rocky cliffs. Some are extremely dangerous because of their deadly venom. Pythons, which may reach 22 feet (6.7 meters) in length, are constrictors. Pythons wrap their bodies around their victim until the prey suffocates.

The venomous black-and-white banded sea snake is one of the few species of sea snakes that comes out of the water to rest and breed. They should definitely be avoided, but there are many other beautiful forms of life under the seas that surround Papua New Guinea.

Divers come from all over the world to marvel at the variety of underwater nature. Coral reefs are gardens of beauty, and not far

The tree frog (top left), the parrot fish (above left), and the starfish (right) are some of the vibrantly colored wildlife.

offshore whales, dolphins, sea rays, and other interesting marine life have found the warm waters abundant with food.

The noted French marine naturalist, Jacques Cousteau, brought his diving crew to the rivers and coral reefs of Papua New Guinea in 1988 to photograph a record-breaking number of unknown sea creatures. They planned to spend a month. They stayed a year.

Huge crocodiles live in the rivers. Although they are worshiped by some groups, they are still caught for their skin and for food. Brave young hunters wade out into the muddy streams armed only with sharp pointed sticks and rope nooses to catch their prey. Some species of crocodiles have been measured at more than twenty feet (six meters) in length. Their teeth are razor sharp. They will eat almost any kind of food that comes their way. There is also a smaller tree-climbing crocodile that lives only in Papua New Guinea. Brilliant-colored tree frogs are another surprise.

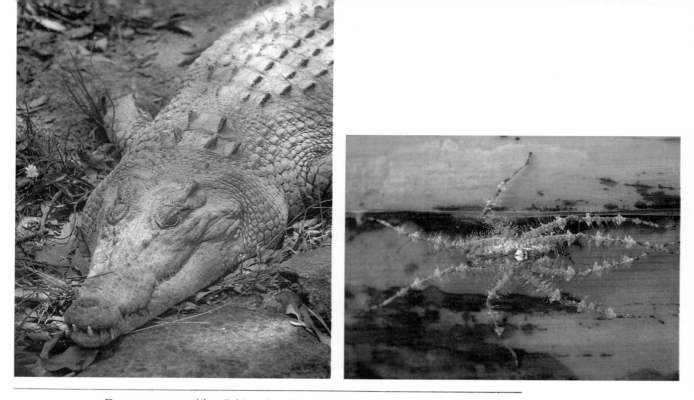

Dangerous crocodiles (left) and spiders (right) abound in Papua New Guinea.

The various insects of Papua New Guinea are probably the least appreciated form of life. There are literally thousands of creepy, crawly specimens that may be beautiful to examine from photographs, but should be avoided in the jungle when possible. Spiders may be exceedingly poisonous. Mosquitoes bring more than just a sting; malaria frequently brings death to the unprotected.

At times butterflies blanket the trees at the edge of the forest with their own confetti of color. Today there are butterfly farms where families raise exotic species and sell mounted specimens to collectors worldwide. The world's largest, called the Queen Alexandria, is the size of a small bird.

Papua New Guinea is a country of beauty and yet a place where people have learned to live under conditions most would consider extremely harsh.

People from the Trobriand Islands (top and bottom left) and a highlander (right)

Chapter 2

THE PEOPLE

The people of Papua New Guinea are as diverse as their country. It is impossible to describe the lifestyle of one village and say it is typical of all. The fact that at least seven hundred different languages or dialects have been recorded in Papua New Guinea shows how cultures developed individually.

Papua New Guineans include brown-skinned pygmies; blue-black, six-foot warriors; bearded highlanders; and hook-nosed lowlanders. There are mountaineers with abnormally strong leg muscles and swamp dwellers who have difficulty walking on solid land because they have become so accustomed to the motion of a canoe.

Most Papua New Guineans living along the coast are a mixture of races, there having been considerable contact in trade and agriculture with seafaring neighbors. Pacific Island racial groups are ranked in three classifications: Polynesian, Micronesian, and Melanesian, but their ancestors, in turn, were a mix of at least four racial groups.

The terms used by anthropologists are: Negritoids, also ancestors of African blacks; Ainoids, ancestors of the early

A large variety of racial groups live in Papua New Guinea.

Australian aborigines and easily recognized by their heavy brow ridges; Veddoids, who were lighter skinned, wavy haired, with similarities to the early people of India; and Mongoloids, noted for their flatter noses and Asian slant of eyes. Micronesians and Polynesians are more closely related to the last group, while the Melanesians of Papua New Guinea are descendants of the Ainoid line.

The origins of these racial groups are uncertain. Papuans, who inhabit the interior of the island, were the first humans to arrive, possibly as long ago as fifty thousand years into the past. Melanesians are believed to have migrated from southeast Asia via the Indonesian islands shortly after the last glacial period, some ten thousand years ago.

Also living in Papua New Guinea today are Australians, Europeans, and a few Americans. They are often the merchants, mining experts, teachers, doctors, and missionaries. Chinese, who arrived late in the nineteenth century to work on the plantations owned by whites, have stayed on as business people.

English is widely used as the official language of the government, but a strange mixture of language called pidgin English is the universal language that helps pull various ethnic groups together.

Melanesia means "Islands of the Blacks." Many Papua New Guineans share Ainoid physical traits, but their ways of life may differ considerably, depending on where they live and the method they use to obtain their food.

DOBU ISLANDERS

Probably the most complicated set of family rules is observed by the Dobu Islanders off the southern shores of Papua New Guinea. Because they have limited physical resources in their environment, there is a jealous regard for property. In some villages inheritance is regulated by the relationships of the wife's family.

Nearly all property, including house sites, land for farming and the trees growing on it, valuable yam seeds, canoes, magical formulas, burial sites, and even the corpses of family members, belong to a woman and her children, together with her brothers and sisters and their children. Children may not inherit any of their father's property; instead they inherit the possessions of their maternal uncle. When they die their property goes to their sister's son or daughter; their bodies will remain with and be interred in their maternal relatives' burial site.

An aerial view of the winding Sepik River and a village situated on the Sepik (left)

SEPIK RIVER–THE RIVER OF ART

Sepik people live in fairly large villages, some of them housing as many as a thousand. Sepik dwellings are more like apartment houses, accommodating two or three families of brothers and their wives. The dwellings are built on stilts to protect against flooding and are apt to be dark and smoky inside, a method of discouraging the clouds of mosquitoes that infest the swamp. The people spend their nights in large basketlike hammocks, tightly woven to keep out insects.

Large houses are usually built in parallel lines facing a cleared space of ground where dances and ceremonial festivals are held. Here is where the sacred spirit house, or *haus tambaran*, is located. These spirit houses are impressive structures that jut high in the

Only men are allowed to enter the spirit house (left). Young men meditate (right) before their initiation ceremony.

sky like the prow of a ship. The roofs are thatch. Decorative wooden panels surround the small entrance doors. The panels are painted and carved with faces representing ancestral spirits and the totem or animal being that represents the clan.

Only men may enter the spirit houses. Within these secret lodge halls are kept all the magical and sacred items that the men believe control their destinies. It is thought that the voices of their ancestors are heard during religious ceremonies. Only their spiritual leaders can hear these voices. The words are interpreted for the village.

Young men undergo a painful initiation ceremony when they come of age. Their heads are shaved and their whole bodies are marked with intricate patterns of cuts, which in turn are treated with herbs to make them fester into heavy welts. It may take the

This crocodile carving adorns a spirit house.

young men several months to recover from the ordeal, but they will then display the ornamentation with great pride. At the same time they will be taught the clan secrets. The young men then will participate in men's affairs and shun the activities of females and uninitiated boys.

Travelers through this area are familiar with the strange froglike call used as a warning by the people of the upper Sepik. It consists of two notes. The first person to raise the alarm keeps repeating the same note until answered by a second person. These two keep the call going, one on the first note, the other on the second. Everyone within hearing takes it up, and in almost no time the countryside seems to echo with the croaking of gigantic frogs.

Other carvings made by the Sepik River people (left)
and some of their pottery (right)

Most villagers believe their people are descended from ancient animals or plants. This belief is woven into the artwork. In one area it was told that men had been swallowed by crocodiles and had been reborn as crocodile men. Carvings of these huge beasts are seen everywhere.

Everything used in daily life is lavishly decorated: spirit masks, shields, canoe prows, musical instruments, bowls, and cooking pots. The Sepik River people believe that the world around them is dominated by hidden spirits. They pay homage to these spirits in their art and ceremonies. It is said that this is the richest source of primitive art in the world. The Sepik River has been called "The River of Art."

Selling betel nuts at a village market

THE NOGULLOS

The Nogullos to the north have an unusual mode of greeting. One extends the knuckle of the middle finger, and the other person grasps the finger between the knuckles of the second and third fingers. When the hands are separated, a loud popping sound can be heard.

Chewing betel nuts is a habit. Villagers carry a knit bag with a supply of green nuts, a gourd filled with lime powder that acts as a catalyst to heighten the effect of the narcotic, and several sprigs of a variety of pepper plant that, when chewed with the nut-lime mixture, seems to soften the acrid taste. The villagers' teeth turn black from the constant use of the betel nuts.

Toniva Beach on Bougainville Island

BOUGAINVILLE ISLAND

Inhabitants of this large island are known as efficient farmers and ambitious traders, with strong family ties. Like the Dobuans, children belong to their mother's clan and may not marry anyone from this clan.

Leadership cannot be inherited. The leader, or *mumi*, reaches that position in a very complicated ceremonial way. He acquires wealth by his own labor, or he can persuade relatives and friends to extend loans to him. One way to earn wealth is to cultivate large gardens and use surplus taro, a root crop, to fatten pigs. The pigs can then be sold for shell money, which is used as currency. Pottery made by the leader's wife also can be sold. Still another way to prosper is to be a professional *shaman*, or diviner, who claims to know the secrets of magic.

What the leader does with his wealth is most important. He must share it by giving lavish feasts, to which he will invite his

*Roasted pigs, potatoes, and other food are being
taken from an underground oven at a village feast.*

whole village and sometimes even his neighboring clansmen. In
this region, food served at a feast includes roasted and steamed
pork, boiled eel and opossum, tasty vegetables, and nut puddings.
A feast provides a welcome break in the day-to-day monotony of
a vegetarian diet and ensures that invitations will be accepted by
everyone. The leader generally makes the feast the occasion for a
house-raising or some kind of work bee, where all put in a bit of
labor.

When a mumi dies, his body is placed on a log bier and
cremated when the morning star appears over the horizon.
Relatives and friends must now give a feast so that he will find
happiness in his afterlife.

To help in the process of setting a bride price, an interesting
custom has evolved. To establish goodwill between the two
families, the groom's people offer somewhat more than they can
afford, and the bride's people return half of what they receive.

Opposite page: A money tree is part of a bride price.

Wig men of the Southern Highlands take part in a sing-sing.

SING-SINGS

Sing-sings are carried on in various villages. They may celebrate a variety of events, from seasonal feasts to initiation rites to marriage.

The dances are almost always an enactment of some dramatic event. Men and women transform themselves into trees, birds, animals, or mountain spirits. Stories of hunts and battles are retold in pantomime.

Asaro mud men

Elaborate body paint, masks, and headdresses are all part of the ritual. Asaro mud men, members of a small group living in the Asaro Valley, wear pumpkin-size clay masks and coat themselves in pale mud to signify death. The Huli wig men from the city of Tari, which is north of Mount Bosavi, weave the hair of their ancestors with fur of the cuscus, daisies, and grass to form enormous headpieces.

THE HIRI OR TRADING VOYAGES

Long ago before the introduction of motorized trading vessels and metal saucepans, there were regular times of the year when *hiri,* or trading voyages, were undertaken. The Motuans who live in the area around Port Moresby made excellent clay cooking pots. They took the pots on voyages and exchanged them for sago in the villages where sago palms flourished.

The voyages were scheduled when the prevailing winds were blowing in a favorable direction. This was during the months when nothing was growing in the gardens of the Motuans and the big fish they caught were far out to sea. The trips lasted for three or four months, and some hiri were for distances of more than 1,000 miles (1,609 kilometers).

The hiri were highly significant events, dominating much of the calendar throughout the year. The practical incentive for undertaking the hiri in the old days was to alleviate the annual food shortage and the threat of famine during the dry season. A complicated ritual of formalities grew up around the event. A mystical social system became interwoven with the practical plan of supplying food. The arrangement affected the very spacing and number of births in the village, because almost all able-bodied males took part in the voyage. It was also a chance for young men to find brides and avoid intermarriage among members of immediate families.

Canoes were built according to strict ceremonial procedure. The canoes were called *lakatoi.* The man chosen to direct the building of the canoes was known as the *baditauna,* "big leader." His partner was the *doritauna,* who was in charge of selecting the mainmast. While canoe building was in progress, the wives of the

The large, sail-equipped canoes, used as trading vessels, were built according to strict ceremonial procedure.

baditauna and the doritauna could only speak to their husbands through a third party and never referred to their husbands by name. Husband and wife had to sleep at opposite ends of the house. These two men became mystically set apart from the village. The two leaders no longer washed themselves or cut their hair. Much of their normal food became taboo.

In August the building began. Four large logs were hollowed out and lashed together to be used as hulls. Before any more building took place, the shaman was called to protect the boat with his magic smoke. The smoke was made from selected herbs and the parings of the claw of the cassowary and the bony snout of a garfish. After the hulls were thoroughly fumigated, small bits of the burned incense would be placed in the hole that held the mainmast.

Next decking was added to cover all four logs, and a square roofless container was built to store the pots to be traded. A lean-to was set at each end of the craft to shelter the crew. As soon as these were ready, the two leaders went aboard. They would live on the ship until the voyage was completed. Each man selected a young boy, usually a son or a sister's son, as his servant and pupil. He was called the *iduha*.

Before there was canvas for sails, women braided strips of palm fronds. Men sewed the final strips together and bound the edges with bark fibers. From the top of each mast hung the clan badge or totem, often a cone shell decorated with a tassel of split leaves. When the trip was over these would be hung from the top of the leader's house.

August was often a month of drenching rain when giant gray-green waves came rolling in across miles of ocean, making coastal sailing dangerous. Therefore, September was usually the month for departure. The pots and emergency food would be stored aboard and there would be a great ceremonial feast on the day the sailors left.

The wife of the baditauna would hang a cord of twisted vines from the rafters of her home. Every ten days she would make a knot in the cord. Until her husband came home she would not cut her hair or go out of her house. She kept the hearth fire burning, because if it died out it was thought that disaster would befall the crew.

After fifty days had passed, a lookout was placed on watch along the highest part of the coast. The people knew the boat could not make the return trip until the trade winds had changed to the northeast. All was planned in anticipation of its return. The village was swept clean of brush. A fattened animal was prepared for the return banquet. When the crew reached their home port, they washed themselves, cut their hair, and rubbed their skin with coconut oil. The sago blocks were brought ashore and stored for

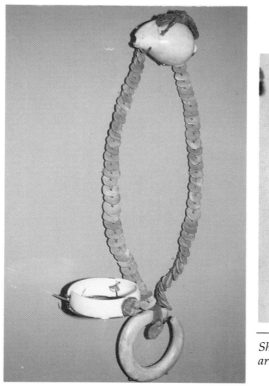

Shell jewelry (left) made from sea animals and armbands (above) made from turtle shells

future use. Lifestyles have changed along the coast. The last hiri took place at Port Moresby in 1940. The people still trade for sago, but more frequently it is a cash transaction or the pots have been replaced with other trading goods.

THE KULA RING

An unusual trading practice was called the kula ring. It linked together groups of islanders who otherwise might have spent their days feuding. As a kind of elaborate peace treaty, twice-yearly voyages were made from island to island with elaborate exchanges of seemingly useless goods. Shell necklaces, called *bagi*, and shell arm bands, called *nwali*, were presented with a formal commitment of friendship.

The shells originally came from the waters surrounding Rossel Island. The women painstakingly ground the red-edged shells into matching circles. Then center holes were drilled and the shells strung in necklaces with lengths of 6 feet (1.8 meters) or more. The necklaces were for display and not to be worn.

Those accepting the gifts displayed their wealth for a few months, then packed up the same presents to be presented to the next island. At times a new, particularly elaborate necklace might be added, but for the most part the same gifts circulated for generations. To keep a sacred piece of jewelry too long was to risk grave danger. Necklaces moved clockwise from island to island, armbands counterclockwise. Within five years the gifts made the complete island circuit. Elaborate ceremonies developed around these various trade goods. This trading system was very important.

TREATIES TO PROTECT TRADE

There was little trade among the inland people, not only because of the difficult terrain but also because of the warlike nature of the people who lived in the mountainous areas. Sometimes sea salt and dried fish from the coast were brought to inland villages by way of the jungle trails. It was a lengthy journey, and trading goods passed from one group to another only after complicated negotiations where the middleman stood to share in the profits.

Later, when steel axes began to find their way to the interior, the inland people still were unaware of the rest of the world. The goods had been handled by so many people that the origin of the merchandise was lost in a jumble of tales.

Until 1933 seashells were the main form of currency. Even today a bride price is usually counted in the size of the great golden-edge clamshells the groom must produce. Cash currency came into use at the beginning of the twentieth century. Laborers in gold mines and on plantations received paper currency, although many refused to accept the paper until they were shown how to exchange it for goods in the trading stores. Until then subsistence farming, hunting, and fishing had always supplied their needs.

RELIGION

Belief in the supernatural has always played a powerful role in the lives of Papua New Guineans. In the minds of the people inanimate objects such as plants, trees, mountains, and rivers often have miraculous powers. Some animals, like the crocodile, are worshiped. Many taboos must be followed to keep the good spirits happy. Each village has its own set of rules, which even today are recognized.

Traditionally, many Papua New Guinean groups had their own beliefs in the gods of good and evil. The Mangen and Mamusi (in the highlands) worshiped Nutu, the Master of All Things. They believed that Nutu made humans and placed a *kanu*, "soul," inside their *lona*, "liver." In death the liver rotted, but the soul went to live with Nutu.

Saia is believed to be the evil one who causes accidents, sickness, and death. Saia can take possession of a common item such as a rotted tree branch and cause a climber to fall. It is believed that Saia actually becomes part of the tree, causing the accident because the injured one has not properly asked for protection.

There is also the belief that some humans have magic powers and can place spells on others. There are confirmed reports that

These science students are studying pineapple extract (above) and sea shells (right) at a private mission school.

people actually have been "scared to death" because they believed that a sorcerer had the power of life and death. A victim simply refused to eat and prepared for his or her end.

Christian missionaries came to the islands shortly after explorers mapped the area in the nineteenth century. They did not push inland very far on the big island of New Guinea. They established missions at trading posts. In the late 1930s Christian missionaries of several denominations followed the gold miners into the highlands. They set up schools and dispensed rudimentary health care. Their main goals were to spread the word of Christianity and to improve living conditions for their converts. Sometimes in their zeal the missionaries destroyed the original culture they were trying to protect.

Before World War II ten mission posts in the highlands between Kainantu and Mount Hagen were directed by Europeans, and seventy-four were managed by local mission teachers.

The Papua New Guinean airline is Air Niuguini.

Unfortunately the Australian government of the Trust did not provide any comprehensive health or education program.

One of the first missionary groups to make permanent contact with people in the highlands after the war was the Missouri Synod of the Lutheran church. As well as teaching Christianity, many families from the United States brought health care and set up schools and agricultural training for the people. Today in the Enga Province near Mount Hagen in the center of the country, more than 60,000 members of this mission make up an active minority among the 200,000 inhabitants of the area. The Lutheran mission's most ambitious project was to build an airstrip at Hewa in the midst of the most difficult terrain, bounded by mountains, dense forest, and huge boulders. One small farm tractor was brought in by helicopter, piece by piece. Supervised by three Westerners, hundreds of local inhabitants accomplished this tremendous job. Women dug around the larger rocks with sticks.

A woman shapes a clay bowl (left) and another woman weaves a new basket from palm fronds (above).

Men attached ropes made of vines and pulled house-size rocks away from the staked-out runway. Even children helped by collecting small pebbles from a nearby stream bed to pave the surface.

The first plane to land arrived in August 1991. This lifeline with the outside world brings in provisions and has airlifted critically ill patients to Port Moresby where they can receive more sophisticated medical help. The most important lesson taught was that local inhabitants could learn to work together; with "one stone at a time" they made the impossible happen.

Today more than 3 million Papua New Guineans claim to be Christian, but their early traditional beliefs continue to be important to them as well.

ART BY WOMEN

Women are involved in some of the craft work, which supplies useful and decorative items. Whereas the Motuans were known

Biliums *are used for toting all sorts of things—even babies.*

for their pottery, the women of Devon on the coast make baskets of all sizes. In the highlands string is made from the bark of the hibiscus plant. The string is used to make fringed skirts, the only clothing in fashion near Mount Hagen in Enga Province. String bags, known as *biliums,* are used to carry everything from produce to firewood. The women of the Kukukuku clan, living in the northern valleys of the mountains, make cloaks of beaten bark for protection from bad weather.

SWEET POTATO AND YAM CROPS

Plants that dominate the lives of many families living in the interior of Papua New Guinea are the sweet potato and yam, related plants that vary greatly in size and texture. The sweet potatoes are similar to what we see in our grocery stores, but certain strains of yams can grow to giant size and have a symbolic meaning—that they give virile strength as well as nourishment to whoever eats them. Trees are cut, underbrush

Yams for sale at the public market in Rabaul

burned, and sprouts from the previous crop are planted in the loose soil with digging sticks. This is considered women's work.

At one time the people planted gardens with a variety of edible crops that flourished the year round, but about three hundred years ago sweet potatoes were introduced. They were easier to grow and pigs liked to eat them raw. Today the people of the Nembi Plateau have specialized in this crop.

In some areas the villages move every few years when the soil has been overworked. In other areas, villages remain where they have been for generations, but gardens may be at a distance until the soil near the village has regained its strength.

Yams are important to the Abelam group of people, who live on the southern slopes of the Prince Alexander Ranges in the Sepik District. They are artistic, noted especially for their beautiful *tamaran*, or cult houses. The roofs of these structures sometimes soar as high as a hundred feet (thirty meters) in the air.

The Abelam are noted for the ceremonial gardens that are

planted with yams. Ceremonial gardens are planted with no more than thirty plants. Women are rigidly excluded from these small gardens. With careful cultivation these tubers sometimes grow to a length of 12 feet (3.6 meters). After the tubers are dug up, they are carefully cleaned by hand and taken to special storage houses in the village. There the yams are kept until required for eating or for planting four to six months later.

Yams are a staple food that stores well for long periods. They represent a kind of cultural currency. A man's accumulation of yams is the measure of his wealth. Symbolic meanings also are given to them. A couple eats a yam together to announce their marriage.

HARVESTING SAGO

The staple food of the Sepik River people is sago from the sago palm, which grows in shallow, freshwater swamps. The trees reach a height of thirty to forty feet (nine to twelve meters) with a diameter of some twenty to thirty inches (fifty-one to seventy-six centimeters). They grow in natural clumps, but harvesters also plant their own stands with green seedlings. The broad-leaved fronds are used for thatching roofs, and the trunks are used for building fences and houses.

Sago is popular, easy to harvest, and has always been an item of trade, although from a nutritional point of view, sago is a poor food. It is high in calories, but has little protein or vitamins.

Each tree takes ten to fifteen years to mature. It then produces a huge flower that rises straight from the top of the palm. Sago eaters cut the palm tree just before it flowers. The logs are either floated or dragged to the village, where women take over the

Making sago flour into cakes for future use

final preparation of the product. The bark is first stripped, exposing the fibrous pith of the palm. The women hammer the pith with a blunt club until it is a fine, fibrous sawdust. This is placed in a sloping trough made from the leaf stalk of the sago frond. The pith is soaked and kneaded like bread dough. Finally more water is added, and the pith is forced through a woven sieve that separates the fine sago flour from the woody pith. After draining the water, the flour is wrapped in leaves and allowed to dry into hard cakes, the final product. This can be kept for several months without spoiling. When it is used, the cake is soaked and cooked like a kind of pancake.

Few other crops are grown, and there is very little meat. When a hunt is successful, the meat is shared.

HUNTING AND FISHING

In the past, the only wild game hunted for food were wild pigs, wild dogs, tree kangaroos, wallabies, and bandicoots. Small

Fishing with a bow and arrow

game used to be caught by setting fire to the grasslands during the dry season, a custom that destroyed much of the native growth. Today there are laws against this practice but few police to see that the laws are observed.

Many species of birds are hunted for food. It takes great skill with a bow and arrow to bring down game in jungle growth. The exception is the cassowary, a flightless bird and a distant cousin of the ostrich, but they have been so extensively hunted they are close to extinction.

On most of the larger river tributaries, crocodiles abound. They grow to enormous size. One catch can provide enough meat for a whole village.

Along the coast and particularly on the smaller islands, fishing is the means to provide food. Papua New Guinea's waters and rivers contain a great variety of edible fish as well as prawns, crayfish, crabs, and other shellfish.

There are many fishing methods. Some fishers use bows and arrows, and others use spears, lines, nets, or large wickerwork

These unusual wickerwork traps are used to catch fish.

traps that look like huge baskets. Smaller traps are made of thorn-covered branches shaped like a cone. Bait is fastened inside the cone, and the trap is lowered on a line to hang just above the river bottom. Fish get caught on the thorns and are retrieved once a day by the fishers.

An even more unusual method is used by the kite fishers. Early in the morning the men go out into the brush collecting spider webs. They attach rolls of the webs to the tail of a kite made of leaves. Paddling offshore they sail their kite just above the water so that the bait skips across the waves, acting as a lively lure. When a large garfish, thinking the bait is a flying fish, bites the bait, its teeth get caught in the web, and the kite is then reeled in.

An easier, less sporting way to land a catch is with a mild poison called rotenone, which is collected by pounding the root of the derris vine. When rotenone is poured into the water, the respiratory system of the fish is paralyzed. When the fish surface they are collected in nets by waiting fishers.

The shores and waters of Papua New Guinea are still littered with live ammunition from World War II. Fishers have been

A local fishing boat near Port Moresby (left) and a sea cucumber (right), an important catch for commercial fishers

known to blow up some of the outer reefs to stun the fish. Great damage has been done to the underwater life of the area. In the last decades of the twentieth century strict rules have been put into practice, but many culprits are not caught.

Fish are extremely rich in protein, which is generally lacking in the diet of most of the Papua New Guineans who live inland. The government is attempting to overcome this deficiency by building fish ponds where farmers can grow their own catch. More extensive trading of fish to inland villages also has been attempted, but lack of refrigeration hampers any large-scale trade. Only fish that have been salted and dried can be traded.

Commercial fishers have found three products that can be exported abroad. One is the sea cucumber, which is related to the starfish, but looks like a cucumber. Sea cucumbers are dried and sold in large numbers to Japan and Malaysia, where they are considered a delicacy.

A small green snail is much sought after by the Japanese for food. Collecting shells that are made into decorative mother-of-pearl items used to be a lucrative business, but pearl buttons are

no longer as popular as they once were. Today plastic resins are often substituted for the real thing.

SPORTS, MUSIC, AND ART

Spear throwing and archery with miniature weapons are more than play for young boys. It is their training for manhood. Tracking small game can be a competitive sport, and boys are trained for the hunt as soon as they can walk.

Girls are not included in sports. They learn their adult roles by taking care of younger children and by helping with the harvest. Organized celebrations in which whole villages gather for a sing-sing take the place of other recreation. There is dancing and chanting to a rhythm beat out on drums. An occasional reed flute is added to the music. Some gatherings last two or three days, ending only when the participants drop from exhaustion.

Living in a climate where wood and fabric easily rot, there is little permanence in Papua New Guinean art. Perhaps because of this, the people use their own bodies as canvases for intricate decoration. Some groups scar their skin in bold patterns. Others paint their bodies in bright colors. Headdresses of brilliant plumage are works of art. Some rituals call for masks that create awe. Shields are decorated with lavish designs, and groups living on river waterways often have master craftsmen who carve the prows of boats with patterns to designate the group of the owner.

The Papua New Guineans are a creative people. Recently some of their masterpieces have made their way to Western museums. There are sculptures in wood, sometimes decorated with shells or crocodile teeth. Pictures of meeting houses show skill in building with only the simplest tools and material.

Opposite page: These dancers use their bodies as canvases to paint. A target for an archery contest (inset), in which first prize was a pig.

Chapter 3

VISITORS TO NEW GUINEA

The first recorded visitors to New Guinea were not Europeans but Indonesians. In the eighth century A.D. a king of Sumatra presented the emperor of China with two dwarfs, a number of parrots, and some Seng-k'i slaves. *Seng-k'i* meant "dark, fuzzy-haired people" in the Malaysian language of Sumatra. The slaves were imported to serve only royalty.

Another mention of the land of New Guinea was recorded as early as A.D. 1365. A poet from Java mentioned two territories as belonging to the Indonesian kingdom of Majapahit. It is doubtful that the territory was explored, but it was important to make the claim to keep rivals from expanding their own rule to the islands to the east.

The discovery of New Guinea by Europeans was bound to happen. Spain and Portugal were rivals for trade in the spice islands of Maluka to the west of New Guinea. The first white men to set foot on the island of New Guinea landed there by accident when their ship was blown off course. Jorge de Meneses, a Portuguese governor of Maluka, reported on their misadventure, and he was not impressed by what he saw in 1526-1527. The land was infested with insects, and there seemed to be no natural crops, especially spices that would encourage further exploration. He called the land *Iihas dos Papuas,* the "land of the fuzzy-haired people" or "Papua."

During the next twenty years the north coast of New Guinea was sighted and roughly mapped by several Spanish captains. It was not officially named until Ynigo Ortiz de Retes, returning from the spice islands to Mexico in 1545, decided to call it *Nueva Guinea.* "New Guinea." It is thought he named it this because of a resemblance between the local inhabitants and those found on the Guinea coast of Africa. The name appeared for the first time on a world map in 1569.

Even with an official title on sailing charts, the landmass was ignored by most explorers. It was not on a direct route used by most of the sailing galleons on their way between Asia and the New World and between Asia and Europe.

SPANISH CLAIMS

One of the few who did record his landing was the Spaniard Luiz Vaez de Torres, who visited Mainu Island in 1606. Torres then sailed west through the strait that now bears his name. This proved that the island was not part of Australia as had at first been thought. Torres annexed the land for Spain, but little was done to officially recognize the acquisition. Spain was busy with problems closer to home. Spanish sea power had greatly declined, and much of the profitable Eastern trade had been taken over by rivals. The most significant voyages around the island now were being made by Dutch, French, Portuguese, and British ships.

BRITISH CLAIMS

The earliest attempts to set up a trading center for spices, if any were to be found, and timber took place in 1793. The location for the settlement was at the western end of New Guinea near the site of Manokwari in present-day Irian Jaya in Indonesia. The area was declared a possession of Great Britain by Captain John Hayes of His Majesty's navy.

Hayes's crew set about building a fortlike settlement with a labor force of some five hundred local inhabitants. The structure was christened Fort Coronation and was governed by fourteen Englishmen and their eleven crewmen from India. The local inhabitants had been frightened into submission by a display of the effects of gunpowder. Retaliation with bows and arrows was not practical, although revenge was not long in coming.

The British crew discovered some trading products of value. There were nutmeg trees, dyewood roots, and teak.

When things seemed to be in order, Captain Hayes set sail for India to bring back supplies and some English settlers. His ship, the *Duke of Clarence,* was swept far off course, not by a storm at sea, but by the political storms of the day. Britain had declared war on France, and Captain Hayes was ordered to put into port at the Chinese harbor of Canton.

Hayes knew his men back in New Guinea were in need of supplies not available from the land they occupied. So he searched until he found someone else to complete his mission. He urged another sea captain, John McCluer, to sail back to Fort Coronation to rescue the men left behind. By the time McCluer arrived, late in 1794, the garrison almost had been wiped out. The monsoon season had flooded them out. The stockade had been attacked by the local people and some of the crew had been captured. There had been several deaths from fever. Those remaining were ready to go home.

The British had now declared war against the Dutch. The British East India Company that handled all trade in the East for England forbade any further settlement in the area, knowing it would be impossible for Britain to defend such a position. The fort was abandoned.

THE DUTCH TRY

The next settlers to try occupying the island were the Dutch, who took possession of the southwest coast of New Guinea in 1828. They founded a government post near Triton Bay. They named their post Merkusoord after the governor of the Malukas. Its little stone fort was called Fort du Bus. As had happened before, the Europeans were almost wiped out by malaria, and the fort was abandoned in 1835. The Dutch kept a claim on the land but were too far away to check on the territory

MARITIME TRADERS

Maritime traders based in Australia were interested in the Pacific islands. Whalers and sealers came first. (Before the development of petroleum products, whale oil was an important commodity.) Traders came in search of pearls, pearl shells, tortoiseshell, sandalwood, ebony, wild rubber, and coconut. They obtained these by trading hatchets, beads, mirrors, rum, and sometimes firearms and ammunition.

Copra, dried coconut meat, was used by Europeans in making

The meat in the center of the coconut is copra.

soap. Soon the demand for Pacific copra outran the supply from the wild groves by the seashore. Europeans moved in and acquired land by purchase or seizure.

Only an occasional small Australian trading vessel made regular stops on the south coast of New Guinea in the 1840s. In 1846 Lieutenant Charles Yule, in a ship called *Ramble,* made a leisurely examination of the coast and took possession of it in the name of Queen Victoria of Great Britain. The British government showed marked indifference toward the annexation. It had already acknowledged Dutch claims to sovereignty over the western half of the island without an argument. It still could not see New Guinea as a profitable area for the British.

THE ARRIVAL OF MISSIONARIES

Christian missionaries landed on the island of Mansinam in Dorei Bay, which is part of present-day Irian Jaya. They were later joined by other missionaries of the Utrecht Mission Society, but in 1864 a severe earthquake and tidal wave destroyed all their

A nineteenth-century mission station at Port Moresby

buildings, and smallpox and dysentery added to their troubles. The mission was closed.

The London Mission Society established teachers on islands in the Torres Strait in 1871, and by 1884 Polynesian pastors had arrived in the Gulf of Papua. Methodist missionaries arrived on New Britain, and the first indigenous (native) pastors were graduated by the London Missionary Society in 1884.

In areas where they worked, Christian missionaries introduced new crops, European clothes and ways of life, steel tools, and new leadership styles. Their influence was significant.

THE GERMANS

In 1884 Germany claimed the northeast part of New Guinea and the Bismarck Archipelago as a German protectorate. The Germans set out to put names on the map on the northern side of the mountain range. The great river, known by its own people as the Sepik, was called the Kaiserin Augusta. The river flows north, then east, and slowly coils its way 1,000 miles (1,609 kilometers)

German Chancellor Bismarck

to the Bismarck Sea. In its middle course, with 300 miles (483 kilometers) more to go before reaching the sea, the river spreads itself as wide as a lake. This is where the Germans set up a temporary trading post in 1884.

The German Chancellor Bismarck issued an imperial charter to the New Guinea Kompagnie, entrusting it with the development of whatever territory could be acquired. The making of laws, though, was reserved to the home government in Germany. There was a problem in finding willing Germans to settle where the climate was unpleasant and the food almost inedible, according to their standards. Most resorted to a diet of canned meat that tasted like "pieces of ship's rope boiled in candle grease," one complainer wrote to the home office.

Mosquitoes came in clouds. Although they were considered a pesky nuisance, no one at the time understood that malaria was caused by the pests. There seemed no way to obliterate them. People who stayed on almost invariably were afflicted with malaria seizures.

The first of the German explorers to head upstream was Vice-Admiral Freiherr G. von Schleinitz, who in 1872 managed to negotiate the river 200 miles (322 kilometers) inland. When the river became too shallow, Schleinitz was forced to turn back. Dr. Charles Schraeder was another who tried exploration of a branch of the Sepik. By 1899 the German government relieved the New Guinea Kompagnie of its administrative responsibilities.

RIVALRY BETWEEN COLONIAL POWERS

The Dutch had been the first Europeans to claim sovereignty in New Guinea, but they were the last to follow up their claim for control. They were much too interested in the more profitable islands of the Dutch East Indies (present-day Indonesia).

However, when the Dutch became afraid that the British would make their claim to the entire island of New Guinea a practical fact, the Dutch officially defined their frontier points as 141 degrees east longitude on the south and 141.47 degrees east longitude on the north coast. This practically laid down the Papua New Guinea and Irian Jaya border of today. The political boundaries were drawn through an interior the colonists had never seen.

Meanwhile the British, goaded on by international rivalry, tried to bring order to the land by using the legal system of Australia. Australia had been under British rule for less than a century. The British stepped in to check both the European brutality of slavery and the barbarism of cannibalism and warfare in New Guinea, just a few miles from Australia's northern frontiers. It was a big order. Missionaries had already tried to set up some semblance of Christianity without any real success. It was fear of punishment

Villages away from the coast (above) were not affected by Europeans. In 1884 the British raised their flag at Port Moresby (right).

from outside authorities, not a change of morality, that pacified some villages.

By 1880 the coastal explorers, missionaries, scientists, and traders had barely scratched the surface of the islands. At that time there were only a handful of churchmen and a few European traders scattered along 3,000 miles (4,828 kilometers) or more of unhealthy, tropical coast. Port Moresby, for example, consisted of a church, a mission station, and a store. It had no government, no police, and no doctor.

In 1884 the German government officially notified foreign powers that the German flag would be hoisted over the archipelago of New Britain and the northeast coast of New Guinea. Three days later on November 6, 1884, the British raised their flag at Port Moresby at the urging of the Australians. The Australian colonies were alarmed. They called for a conference to settle boundaries. An agreement was signed in April 1885 that gave Germany some 63,000 square miles (163,170 square kilometers) of northeastern New Guinea and Britain some 60,000 square miles (155,400 square kilometers) in the southeast.

Negotiations to convert the British New Guinea Protectorate into an outright annexation dragged on until 1887. This spurred more newcomers to make their homes in the colony. Gold was discovered in 1888 and brought hundreds of miners to the colony. There have always been two types of immigrants in colonial times: the temporary resident and the settler. Those who came to Papua New Guinea were temporary residents who came for a while to govern or earn a living but had no plans for permanent settlement. In 1888 Britain annexed the territory as the crown colony of British New Guinea.

BRITISH NEW GUINEA

It was the Australians who lent continuity to the government of the country. They tried to raise the standard of living of those they governed. Germans were more apt to import other Asians for plantation labor. For the most part the indigenous population of New Guinea governed by the Australians was the one to benefit by a Western wage scale.

Britain named Sir William MacGregor the first lieutenant-governor in 1888. He was a fair and conscientious man, who tried to limit the unrest in the territory. He also explored much of the area and mapped the coastline and navigable rivers.

MacGregor was succeeded by Sir George LuHunte, who increased his administrative force to fifty officers. But without funds to help the people, Papua, the name given to the British territory, remained a primitive land.

At this time Papua showed many of the worst features of an isolated pioneer frontier in the tropics. Colonialism gave the British, Dutch, Germans, and Australians power. The handful of colonial officials included some who were weak and quarrelsome. Drunkenness among the colonists was prevalent.

Papua New Guineans under colonial control were called *kanakas* and were expected to call all white people, regardless of status, *masta* and *misis*. A New Guinea male was a *boi*. They were expected to stand up when spoken to, obey curfew laws that kept them off the streets at certain times, and to step aside when meeting Europeans on pavements. There was no social intimacy between segregated races.

GERMAN NEW GUINEA

In 1899 German New Guinea was made an imperial colony administered by German government officials. In contrast to the British and Australians in Papua, the Germans mainly developed plantations and a colony for whites, and did little for the indigenous population. By 1914 it was a plantation colony run by white Germans.

CHANGES CAUSED BY WORLD WAR I

Australia became independent of Great Britain in 1901. In 1902 British New Guinea passed to Australian control and was renamed the Territory of Papua in 1906. Hubert Murray was named lieutenant-governor in 1908, a post he held until 1940. He had an enormous impact on Papua during the next three decades.

While most of the military action of World War I took place on European soil and on Atlantic waters, colonial interests spread the conflict to the Pacific. While the war was being fought on other fronts, a German officer was sent out to survey the border

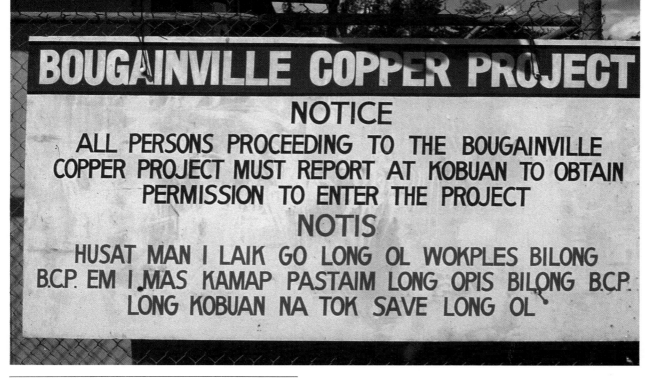

BOUGAINVILLE COPPER PROJECT

NOTICE

ALL PERSONS PROCEEDING TO THE BOUGAINVILLE COPPER PROJECT MUST REPORT AT KOBUAN TO OBTAIN PERMISSION TO ENTER THE PROJECT

NOTIS

HUSAT MAN I LAIK GO LONG OL WOKPLES BILONG B.C.P. EM I MAS KAMAP PASTAIM LONG OPIS BILONG B.C.P. LONG KOBUAN NA TOK SAVE LONG OL

A sign in English and Pidgin English

between German New Guinea and Papua. Captain Herman Detzner kept his flag flying over a remote base until Germany surrendered in 1918. Australian forces were sent to occupy the territories, and Australia was given the right to administer this trust as an integral part of its territory.

In 1921 the former German New Guinea was placed under a League of Nations mandate administered by Australia. It was not united with Papua as a government unit. There were even two different official languages. Motu, a simplified native language, was used by the Motuans in Papua. Pidgin English was used in the Trust. The outsider population consisted of Germans, Chinese, Japanese, and a few British. The gold discoveries in the territories made it considerably richer than Papua, but the great interior was yet to be explored.

A secluded village in the highlands

Chapter 4

FIRST CONTACT

THE HIGHLANDS DISCOVERED

On the morning of May 27, 1930, shortly after dawn, an event took place that will never happen again on earth. Two gold prospectors from Australia and fifteen carriers from the coast walked into a highland valley in the interior of Papua New Guinea and discovered–to their astonishment–a previously unknown civilization of nearly one million people.

It was a frightening experience for both the prospectors and the highland people who were seeing white-skinned humans for the first time. They were sure the white men were ancestral spirits returned from the dead. Their custom of drying the corpses of their relatives turned the skin of the dead to a grayish pallor. This was probably what saved the lives of Michael and Dan Leahy. Strangers were not usually tolerated, even neighboring strangers.

It is truly remarkable that such a large civilization could have remained undetected for so long–four hundred years after the island had been drawn on the world map. Only after the Leahys reported their astonishing encounter did scientists and mining speculators follow their trails inland.

The whole highland zone was not as forbidding as had been thought. Several broad, flat-floored valleys are wedged between the main ridges at heights of 4,000 to 7,000 feet (1,219 to 2,134 meters). Some of these valleys, such as Wahgi, which is 10 miles (16 kilometers) wide, are quite extensive. Grasslands support large populations.

Emerging archaeological evidence suggests the highland New Guineans were among the world's first agriculturalists. Some of them were growing vegetables in gardens drained by ditches at least nine thousand years ago. The malaria mosquito that had limited the lowland population did not survive at the higher altitudes. The highlanders thrived and multiplied. At the time of contact in the 1930s they were among the healthiest, most vigorous people in New Guinea.

Why had it taken so long to find these people? One answer is the lack of wild game or edible wild plants to provide food for explorers. A porter can carry about forty pounds (eighteen kilograms) on his back for long distances, the weight of food needed to feed himself for about fourteen days. Until the advent of planes made airdrops possible, all New Guinea expeditions that penetrated more than a seven-mile (eleven-kilometer) walk from the coast—fourteen days round trip—did so by having teams of porters going back and forth building up food depots inland.

The expedition that came the closest to discovering the Grand Valley, the 1921-1922 Kremer Expedition, used 800 porters and 200 tons (181,440 kilograms) of food and took six months relaying to get four explorers just to the edge of the valley.

The Leahys returned to the highlands many times. They did a

A local guide with some visitors photographed in the 1920s

remarkable job of filming the record of the meetings of these two divergent cultures. It is amazing to think that there are people living today who remember those days of first contact.

Those who came to study these "new" people discovered that the highlanders usually spent their entire lives within twenty miles (thirty-two kilometers) of their birthplaces. They might occasionally enter lands bordering their village lands by stealth during a war raid or by permission during a trading truce, but they had no social framework for travel beyond their immediate neighboring lands. The notion of tolerating unrelated strangers was as unthinkable as the notion that any such stranger would dare appear. Many "precontact" people thought they were the only humans in existence. Some thought the trees on the ridge of hills that blocked their horizon were what held up the sky.

Now that the highlands were known to be inhabited, aircraft and radio assisted in their development. Grasslands were cleared in some of the valleys to make way for landing fields. Suddenly twentieth-century technology came to a Stone Age people.

GOLD

Gold fields were discovered in the Territory of New Guinea highlands at such places as Edie Creek and the Bulolo River area and a gold rush began in 1926. This brought a flood of prospectors from Australia. Some of the fields were in almost impenetrable country, where it took porters weeks to haul in equipment. Finally the Guinea Gold Company successfully replaced Papuan carriers with aircraft. Huge earth-moving machinery was dismantled and transported by cargo planes to mining sites in less than an hour. Air transport revolutionized exploration and development of the country. Gold made the government of the Territory of New Guinea comparatively richer than the government of the Territory of Papua.

WORLD WAR II

In the early 1940s Papua and New Guinea were drawn into a war that engulfed the entire world. In 1941 and 1942 the Japanese won some of the most sweeping military successes of the war. They temporarily crippled European and American sea power in the Pacific and gained control of a large part of eastern and southeastern Asia. Their objectives were to set up a line of island bases from the Aleutian Islands in the far north through Midway Island to the South Pacific, with Port Moresby as the southern outpost. The Japanese were in need of the raw materials southeast Asia had to offer: tin, rubber, and oil.

Japanese forces spread southward rapidly, overrunning the major centers of Allied power in Hong Kong, the Philippines, and Singapore. By January 1942, only a month after their attack on

*The first U.S. fighter plane to arrive in New Guinea
during World War II was a P-38.*

Pearl Harbor, the Japanese had reached the island of New Britain off the coast of the Territory of New Guinea. From there they prepared to conquer Australia.

By February 1942 the Japanese were sending regular bombing raids over Darwin in Australia, Rabaul in New Britain, and Port Moresby. A bitter struggle took place for Guadalcanal, in the Solomon Islands. The Japanese lost this battle but established their headquarters in Rabaul, the capital of New Britain.

In the battle for the Pacific the Japanese hurriedly built scattered airfields across an arc of small islands off the north and northwest coasts of New Guinea. The Australians and Americans built their first airstrips in Milne Bay and on its offshore islands, including the Trobriands. From these bases, the Japanese and the Allied forces took to the air in an attempt to defeat one another in a continuing series of bombing raids that lasted for three years.

Although the Americans had lost much of their fleet at Pearl Harbor, they still possessed enough air power to inflict heavy

This man was one of the many mountain people who helped the Americans and Australians build military roads to carry equipment and supplies.

losses on the Japanese fleet. Decisive sea battles took place in the Coral Sea in May 1942 and at Midway Island in June of the same year.

The Battle of the Coral Sea stopped the Japanese naval takeover of Port Moresby. The Japanese attempted to secure Port Moresby, the defense center, by crossing the almost-impassable Owen Stanley Mountains and landing troops on the Allies' eastern flank at Milne Bay in the extreme southeast of New Guinea. However, the Japanese failed.

For many villagers it was probably never clear why the hordes of strangers had invaded their world or why they were trying to kill one another as they swept across it. The ever-present danger of aerial bombardments and military restrictions on sea travel limited local fishing and caused a temporary halt in the ancient kula ring.

During the war some 55,000 people from Papua and New Guinea served as carriers, laborers, and guides. Often innocent villages were strafed. Both Australians and the people of New Guinea and Papua paid a bitter price for living in the path of the war. The damage to property included destruction of buildings

*A downed Japanese bomber from World War II
has become a planter in the jungle.*

and their contents, canoes, livestock, and useful trees by both
Allied and Japanese bombing. The requisition of livestock and
food by the Japanese and of timber and sago palm leaf by the
Allies caused many hardships.

THE END OF WORLD WAR II AND NEW POLICIES

World War II encouraged the end of European-style colonialism
in Asia. In 1945 Colonel Jack Keith Murray, a former professor of
agriculture at Queensland University in Australia, was appointed
chief administrator of the territories of both Papua and New
Guinea. It was up to him to at least lay the foundations for an
independent government. He was expected to set up health and
education services, control local disputes, and answer to planters,
traders, and miners. The miners complained that it was impossible
for them to make a living unless certain restrictions against land
acquisition and a fixed labor policy were relaxed. The problem
was to keep Europeans in the country by offering them profit
incentives and at the same time to honor pledges that Australia
would safeguard landholdings and respect local customs.

Chapter 5

A NEW NATION

After World War II the rush for independence was on. Australia was anxious to rid itself of some of its costly responsibilities. A joint administration of the Territories of Papua and the Trust Territory of New Guinea had been established by Australia in July 1949. The union was the Territory of Papua and New Guinea.

A Legislative Council was established in November 1951. The Council was replaced by a House of Assembly in June 1964. The territory was renamed Papua New Guinea in July 1971. It achieved independence on September 16, 1975, when the House of Assembly became the National Parliament. Michael Somare, who had served as chief minister in an interim coalition government since 1972, became prime minister on independence.

Many changes have occurred since independence day when Australia's Prime Minister Gough Whitlam and Britain's Prince Charles stood at attention with a crowd of some ten thousand in a Port Moresby sports stadium to watch the exchange of flags that marked the birth of the world's newest nation.

Many people in Australia, the former colonial power, had misgivings. They were sure internal chaos would follow. They feared there would be racial tension because of the various mixtures of ethnic groups that wanted a say in the government.

Prime Minister Michael Somare also may have seen troubled times for the future. But Somare had confidence that ultimately his country could deal with the problems. The economic health of the country was a primary concern. Would foreign capital be available for the development of national resources? The answer has been yes.

The day he took office at the age of thirty-nine, Somare spoke with authority as he raised his fist in salute to his audience. "They said we were a stone-age people, who couldn't think of independence for another fifty years. We have proved them wrong. This is just the beginning. Now we must stand on our own two feet and work harder than ever before."

From the beginning the new government was plagued by two separatist movements. One was led by Josephine Abaijah, who was the only woman in the 109-member Parliament. She fought for the southern region of Papua to break away from the rest of the country and declare its own independence. Her followers, mostly merchants and traders who already had participated in world trade, did not want their wealth shared by the poorer inland sections of the country.

A more serious threat came from the outlying island of Bougainville with its immense open-cut copper mine that was generating fully half of the country's internal revenue. The Bougainville secessionists argued that their island had stronger ethnic and geographic ties to the nearby Solomon Islands, a British protectorate, than to Papua New Guinea.

Only after some intense negotiation, during which the people of Bougainville were given assurance that they would have a strong influence on the affairs of the country, were they finally persuaded to stay within the jurisdiction of the new Parliament. Bougainvillers were told that without a unified country behind them, their chance for future involvement in international commerce would disappear. That same separatist movement was to flare up later.

A great number of the indigenous people did not want unification. The highlanders had lagged behind the coastal people socially, economically, and educationally. They had fewer contacts with the outside world. The highlanders were fearful they would be dominated by those living what was now being called a more advanced lifestyle. There was a problem in creating a sense of loyalty to the government in Port Moresby, which seemed remote from the highlanders and their problems.

There were others who held an opposing viewpoint. In the past there had been a thin veneer of courtesy between the white settlers and indigenous people. Often great resentment was felt by New Guineans that they were being kept from managing their affairs. "You have given us many good things, but you have not taught us how to achieve these things without you," was a thought voiced by many islanders.

A COMMONWEALTH OF NATIONS

Although Papua New Guinea has won independence, technically the new country is still under the shelter of the British Commonwealth of Nations.

Papua New Guinea's executive power is vested in the British monarch, represented locally by a governor-general, who is appointed on the recommendation of Papua New Guinea's prime minister and Cabinet. The governor-general, who must be a citizen of Papua New Guinea, acts for the British monarch as the ceremonial chief of state. The head of government is the prime minister. In spite of the ties to the Commonwealth, New Guinea has the decisive vote in her own affairs.

Legislative power is in the hands of a single National

The Parliament Building in Port Moresby

Parliament, whose members are elected for a period of up to five years. All persons over the age of eighteen are eligible to stand for election and to vote. Voting is by secret ballot. General elections are held at least every five years. The National Executive Council appointed by the prime minister is responsible to the Parliament.

As part of the policy of decentralization, the government established provincial governments in each of the twenty provinces as early as 1978. Local officials represent 90 percent of the population through more than 160 councils.

GOVERNMENT

Papua New Guinea, unlike many other new states, has shown that it understands democracy. Its Parliament is free to challenge the government with a vote of no confidence. Such votes are easily won in a Parliament made up of numerous small parties.

Political parties are based not on ideology but on personality and regional ties. Guided mainly by self-interest, politicians are free to shift from one party to another after they are elected. These ever-shifting alliances produce increasingly frequent changes of government. The prime minister, who is elected on the floor of Parliament and is generally the leader of the majority party, is given six months' grace, after which he or she can be challenged at any time.

In some ways this "instability" based on diversity is a source of stability in Papua New Guinea. No single group is powerful enough to take over, so the sort of coup seen in other countries is unlikely. But it also means direct action is slow in coming. Much time is spent in political maneuvering. Because there are few ideological differences between parties—all basically favor free enterprise—legislation rarely results in change of government policy. Prime ministers with an eye to survival are unable to take tough measures to tackle obstacles to reform.

A governing coalition is formed by mutual agreement among groups with varying interests. Other parties try to lure coalition groups away with promises of a better deal if the opposition comes to power, while the prime minister tries to hold onto them with counter promises.

Michael Somare, the first prime minister, remained in office until 1980, despite widespread allegations of inefficiency in government ministries and of discrimination against the highland provinces. In March 1980 Sir Julius Chan, the leader of the People's Progressive Party, succeeded to the position of prime minister. But Somare became prime minister again in August 1982, following a general election in June.

In 1983 in spite of a general policy of decentralization, the Somare government changed the constitution to provide greater

Left: In the 1970s Prime Minister Michael Somare visited
U.S. Secretary of State Henry Kissinger in Washington, D.C.
Right: Sir Julius Chan became prime minister in 1980 and 1994.

control over provincial governments. It had become evident that some government officials took advantage of their position to fill their own pockets. Money allocated for local services seemed to disappear, and projects were never completed.

In 1985 Deputy Minister Paias Wingti resigned his position and his membership in the Pangu Pati (party) to challenge Somare for the premiership. A no-confidence vote was put before the legislature and Wingti was nominated as alternative prime minister.

Somare quickly formed a coalition made up of the ruling Pangu Pati, the National Party, and the Melanesian Alliance. The no-confidence vote was rejected by 68 votes to 19. Fourteen members of Parliament who had supported the motion were expelled from the Pangu Pati and subsequently formed the People's Democratic Movement under the leadership of Wingti.

The balance of power has seesawed back and forth between a handful of busy politicians. A plan to levy a tax on food imports

Paias Wingti (left) was elected prime minister in 1985, 1987, 1988, and 1992. In July 1992 Rabbie Namalie (right) became Papua New Guinea's fourth prime minister.

caused lengthy debate. Wingti came to power in 1986 by declaring that his aim was to reduce government expenditures rather than raise taxes.

The only hope for a stable government was for opponents to compromise and work together. An amendment to the constitution was finally passed in 1989, whereby a motion expressing no confidence in the prime minister could not be proposed until he or she had completed thirty months in office. It also obliged members of Parliament who changed parties after an election to stand for reelection.

Paias Wingti's government fell in 1988, when the ministers of finance, the treasury, and foreign affairs deserted him in favor of Rabbie Namaliu, who became the country's fourth prime minister.

Mr. Namaliu named a government that included most of the regions and five of the political parties. Somare was persuaded to act as minister of foreign affairs. However, in July 1992 Parliament elected Paias Wingti prime minister with a one-vote margin over his predecessor Rabbie Namaliu.

Sir Julius Chan was elected again in 1994. He has been committed to obtaining peace with revolutionary forces in Bougainville.

Changing the constitution in Papua New Guinea is a tough business. At least seventy-two members have to be persuaded to vote for the change, not only once but twice, at sittings not less than six weeks apart. This gives time for changing sides and dickering with opponents for an exchange of votes on other issues.

CRIME AND PUNISHMENT

The current government has enough local problems to keep it busy. The most pressing problem is how to handle crime in urban communities. Gangs of mostly educated, unemployed youths, known as "rascals," have turned parts of urban centers such as Port Moresby and Lae into violent towns.

Corruption within the government has been a worry since independence. Namaliu was the first prime minister to hold a university degree. He had a good record which Chan continues.

The court system is much like ours, with a judge making some decisions after hearing lawyers speak for both sides of cases. In more serious crimes a jury is selected to decide on guilt or innocence. The last records available show that in 1990 more than 1,500 criminal and civil cases were heard in the National Court and an estimated 120,000 cases in district and local courts. The discretionary use of the death penalty for murder and rape was introduced in 1991.

There is also a separate courtlike body called the Leadership Tribunal, which is appointed by the legislature to investigate charges against elected officials. On September 27, 1991, the Tribunal found the deputy prime minister, Ted Diro, guilty of corruption. When Governor-General Sir Vincent Serei Eri refused to remove his friend from office, both men were forced to resign by order of this legal body.

EDUCATION

New Guinea has more than seven hundred languages, many of them unrelated to any other known language in New Guinea or elsewhere. The average New Guinea language is spoken by a few thousand or even a few hundred people living within a radius of ten miles (sixteen kilometers).

To Europeans there seemed to be no single best local language to use in teaching. Different languages were better suited for different purposes. The only previous form of communication, which had developed along the coast, was Melanesian Pidgin. This had evolved from a vocabulary of a few meaningful English, German, and Malay words strung together in Melanesian grammar patterns. It could be learned speedily by both adults and children of all indigenous linguistic groups. Within weeks it could be used as a means of communication between European and local people and between people who did not know each other's language.

Bitter controversy raged among educators, who were trying to set up some system of standardized schooling for the country. A compromise was reached. In the late 1950s, the 109-member national legislature decided that early grades would be taught in the easier Pidgin, but English would be introduced in secondary school classes. Later evidence proved that it was easier for children to learn English if they started at age seven or eight. But was English all that important?

When Papua New Guineans were first appointed to the

Legislative Council, most of them made their speeches in Pidgin. Court proceedings were ordinarily first given in Pidgin and then translated from Pidgin to English. Administrative orders and pronouncements were published in Pidgin, and it was the language used in the great majority of newspapers and broadcasts.

Some people felt the teaching of English was useless and nonproductive. They thought learning to read and write would be an asset only in a society with a genuine use for the skill. Farmers who were involved in raising food only for their own families and not for a cash market did not need this knowledge, people said. But the Australian-led administration persisted in giving high priority to formal schooling.

In 1950-1951, from a school-age population of about 500,000 in both territories, 132,000 pupils were receiving instruction in subsidized mission schools and about 4,000 in new administration schools. Ten years later the total had risen to 217,000. The rise in school population was not nearly as significant an achievement as figures might seem to indicate. The great majority of pupils left school before they had acquired effective literacy of any kind. In 1961 only 564 children were attending secondary schools and none had yet qualified for university entrance.

Knowing that independence would soon be coming to New Guinea, Australia put on a "crash education" system, sending certain children from the coastal areas to Australia to be educated. It has been said that these select few were the most unfortunate of children, because over a number of years they became conditioned to white economic and social standards, only to be forced in the end to return to a society from which they had been intellectually and emotionally alienated.

A primary school in the Sepik River region

Most of the indigenous families unfamiliar with a written language had great fear and suspicion of such magic that could talk from paper. When disputes were brought to a local council for arbitration, tape recorders were often used to draw up contracts. Hearing their own voices played back seemed more natural to the people, and the tapes could always be played again for future reference in case another member of the group might question the verdict.

Today there are 715 indigenous languages. English is spoken by less than 2 percent of the people, but Pidgin English is widely understood. The language of Motu is spoken in the Papua region.

Progress has been slow, but gradually figures are beginning to mean something. Today six years of education are compulsory. Primary classes taught in community schools begin at seven years of age and last for six years. Free primary education was introduced in 1988. Secondary education, beginning at age

The library of the University of Papua New Guinea

thirteen, lasts for up to six years. In the early 1990s the total enrollment at primary schools equaled 73 percent of children in that age range, and comparable enrollment in more advanced classes was 13 percent. The curricula has been designed to permit students to return to work in the rural areas in which 85 percent of the population live. Literacy was about 52 percent in 1995.

Advanced education is now provided by the University of Papua New Guinea and the Papua New Guinea University of Technology. There are teacher training colleges and higher institutions that cater to specific professional training. The government spends 17 percent of its income on education.

HEALTH SERVICES

Improving public health has been a harder problem. Short life expectancy results from unsatisfactory diet, malaria, intestinal parasites, dysentery, skin infections, and other diseases. Before World War II, medical services in the territory, whether supported by missions or the administration, existed more to protect the health of recruited laborers than to serve the population as a whole. Projected 1990-1995 life expectancy figures for males are 56 years and for females 57.

Drugs and insecticides developed during the war made malaria control possible in theory, but in practice it was impossible to cover such a large and remote part of the landscape. There was greater success in the control of yaws, a highly contagious skin disease, and tuberculosis, because medical patrols gave mass inoculations even in remote areas. Leper hospitals halted the spread of this dread disease. Typhoid, measles, whooping cough, and dysentery also are kept in check, although pneumonia still exacts a heavy toll of deaths.

The government recognizes the need for improved medical care and is paying for the expansion of health services throughout the country. It spends 11 percent of its budget for social services. Christian missions also provide medical and health services with government assistance.

Within urban centers a certain amount of the national budget is set aside for welfare. It is a rather small amount, for there is little unemployment for those with skills. There is a growing crime rate. Poverty is most often the cause. The government is spending money on low-cost housing in Port Moresby and Lae.

Those who have not been able to fit into Western specialized industry and agriculture in urban areas are sent back to the villages they left behind in the country. Families tend to take care of their own in rural areas.

Chapter 6

PAPUA NEW GUINEA IN THE MODERN WORLD

NATURAL RESOURCES

It is said that Papua New Guinea moved from the Stone Age to the Plastic Age faster than any other culture on earth. In the 1990s the country faces another dramatic jolt: a minerals boom on an unprecedented scale.

Gold and copper already account for more than two-thirds of Papua New Guinea's exports. The country's mineral wealth is vast in relation to the size of its population. Oil is the next treasure that has been found and is ready to be exploited.

COPPER

The Panguna copper mine on Bougainville is one of the largest man-made holes in the world. The immense pit was excavated by four-story-high shovels that could scoop 22 tons (19,958 kilograms) of ore in one bite. Dump trucks could carry away 150 tons (136,080 kilograms) of rock in one trip. There were 45 such trucks.

The copper mine in Bougainville

Four thousand people were working the mine in three eight-hour shifts a day before it closed on May 15, 1989. When it was in operation, the mine accounted for 2 percent of world copper production, 45 percent of Papua New Guinea's export earnings, and 17 percent of the national government revenue.

The mine is so wide it would take two Golden Gate bridges to span the hole, and if the Empire State Building were set on the bottom of the hole in a vertical position, it would disappear from view.

The copper deposits were discovered in 1965. When the mine opened in 1972 it trebled Papua New Guinea's annual volume of foreign sales. Most of the ore was bulk shipped to Japan, West Germany, and Spain. Though 80 percent of its profits went to public shareholders and Australian corporate owners, 20 percent remained with the government. Corporate taxes also added to the treasury.

Since 1989 there have been problems that have caused the closure of the rich Panguna mine. Local landowners revolted, and at least fifteen people were killed in violence that was marked by the use of guns as well as bows and arrows. The people who owned the original land are demanding the equivalent of $11.5 billion in compensation for environmental damage.

The government's security force had to be used to keep peace. It is almost impossible to defend the mine and its twelve-mile (nineteen-kilometer) power line that snakes through dense jungle.

On September 11, 1989, Mr. John Bika, a thirty-nine-year-old government official in Bougainville's provincial government, was murdered. He had been scheduled to arrive in Port Moresby the next day to sign an agreement that would have given Bougainville's residents a bigger financial stake in all copper mining carried out on the island. He was killed by people who wanted independence for Bougainville.

The mine had been closed since May 15, 1989, but on September 5 of that year the mine owners were reluctantly persuaded to reopen. Within eight hours it was shut down again after rebels attacked the miners.

The rebel leader, Mr. Francis Ona, a former mine surveyor, wanted secession. The island's people had long sympathized with Ona. Prime Minister Namaliu would have liked to order the army to capture Ona, but that was risky, and conciliation was attempted. Prime Minister Chan has negotiated peace terms with the current revolutionary leader.

Surprisingly the country's budget has been hurt less than might have been expected. Taxes and dividends from mining are not spent as they are received, but are paid into the Mineral Resources Stabilization Fund, of which only part is drawn upon each year. Even though the mine on Bougainville remained closed, there was enough of the fund to see the government through to 1992. Since then taxes from the rich deposits at Ok Tedi have more than balanced the budget. Ok Tedi is literally a mountain of copper with a cap of gold. Only because of the difficulty of transportation and production have the facilities been slow in reaching their potential. The Ok Tedi Copper Mine, operated by an Australian firm, is perched on a remote mountaintop in the highlands. Exploration and development costs are perhaps three times as high as those in Australia, but because the deposits are so rich, operating costs per ton are one-third lower.

The impact of the mine closure in Bougainville had an effect on the country's foreign exchange reserves. Foreign investors lacked confidence to back future developments. In the hopes that any further conflict with local tribal landowners could be avoided, more generous participation was adopted. The original Bougainville deal gave 5 percent royalties to landowners. Under the new national mining policy at Ok Tedi, they receive 20 percent plus the opportunity to become actual shareholders in the mine.

In the new highland mines, jobs and contracts have gone mainly to local residents. This has given them a greater incentive to keep the mine open.

GOLD

Other wealth has been found in unexplored regions. When Porgera Gold Mine, a joint venture of Placer, Renison Goldfields, and MIM Holdings, British and Australian-backed companies, began production in late 1991, it was the biggest gold mine outside South Africa. Another mine on the island of Lihr, a small island to the east of New Britain, is waiting approval, and may be bigger still. Although all equipment must be shipped in by sea, development costs should be lower than in the highlands. If all new mines reach production in the 1990s, gold output will triple and will make Papua New Guinea the third largest gold producer in the world.

AGRICULTURE

The government is talking wisely about the need to develop renewable resources in contrast to what is taken out of the land. Scientific farming could do much to improve living conditions. More than two-thirds of the working population of Papua New Guinea are engaged in subsistence agriculture, growing mainly roots and tubers.

Many people make the mistake of thinking that tropical soils are fertile because of the dense tropical forests they support. In fact, the luxuriant growth of the forests depends on abundant rainfall and a particular cycle of soil enrichment that, when interrupted, leaves the soil very poor.

Nutrients are taken in from the soil by the growing plants of the forest. These plants cannot live without a certain kind of bacteria that is in their roots. The bacteria form nitrogen compounds from nitrogen in the air. These compounds then become available to the plants. To complete the cycle the plant gives food material to the bacteria. The nutrients are later returned to the soil through the forest litter, which combines dead branches, leaves, and animal droppings.

When farmers cut down the forest to make their gardens, they interrupt the cycle of nutrients. Soon the soil is no longer capable of producing food crops. It takes only a year or two for this to

Farmers sell their vegetables and fruits at the local markets.

happen. Then the farmers must abandon their fields for several years and allow them to revert to bush and forest so that nutrients can again build up in the soil.

The forest often looks like a patchwork quilt when seen from the air. In some places people have turned the forest into scrub grassland by cutting too many trees and by burning the underbrush. Without chemical fertilizer to enrich the soil, the land has no hope of returning to forest. The tremendous downpours of rain wash away the natural minerals of the soil.

There are some areas on New Guinea with fertile soils, but other problems keep farmers from developing the land. The land may be too steep in a mountainous area, or too wet around the volcanoes of central Papua, or too dry in the area where the rain disappears into porous rock. It is not an easy country to convert to large-scale agriculture.

There is tremendous pressure to increase production of the main export crops—coffee, cocoa, and palm oil—as farmers shift to cash crops. The problem is that the system of ownership makes it difficult to obtain land for expansion. Some 97 percent of all land is owned by clans under community title and cannot be bought, sold, or leased by individuals.

Under the old system that their ancestors had lived by for generations, land was owned by the community with certain rights being "loaned" to families for their own use. One family might have the right to grow food, another to gather firewood, and another to hunt, gather fruit from certain trees, and collect edible insects. If a stream or river ran through the community property, one family might have the sole right to fish the waters with the understanding they would share their catch in exchange for crops.

Now when land is being planted with new crops that are harvested for cash, violent disputes have broken out between families. The government has had a difficult time registering deeds because most land is owned by family groups.

The expansion of agriculture would help to halt the drift of population into larger towns.

URBAN CENTER–PORT MORESBY

Port Moresby is by far the largest city in Papua New Guinea. In 1970 the population was only a little over 56,000. Today it is home to more than 190,000. Although it has a deep natural harbor and an international airport, Port Moresby has grown, not because of its importance as a commercial center, but because it is the capital and center of government.

Port Moresby

Port Moresby's harbor

The site of the town was discovered by Captain Moresby in 1873 when he was surveying the New Guinea coast. In 1874 the Reverend W.G. Lawes of the London Missionary Society established a mission station near the Montuan village of Hanuabada, situated on the shores of the harbor.

The original town grew up on a headland between the harbor and Ela Beach. This site, facing the harbor, became very congested. After World War II the administration built new headquarters at Konedobu, almost two miles (three kilometers) north of the original town. Residential development spread first eastward from Ela Beach to Koki and, in 1951, inland to the predominantly European suburb of Boroko. More recently,

Ela Beach (above) and Koki village (top right), which is built on stilts as protection from the rising waters and to make the houses cooler

industrial areas have developed that separate the residential suburbs built at Hohola and Waigani.

Port Moresby has attracted a great number of migrants from the interior and from coastal islands. It is essentially a European town with a number of settlements in which the Papua New Guineans themselves are generally grouped on the basis of language and culture. Outside working hours there is very little contact between the various ethnic groups. These migrant settlements provide poor, overcrowded housing and few services. In some cases employers have built low-cost housing for their workers near the factories and businesses they serve, but there are too few such projects.

Rabaul harbor on New Britain Island

THE PORT OF RABAUL

Rabaul, the capital of New Britain, is the country's main port for exports. It serves not only New Britain but also the islands of the Bismarck Archipelago, which are linked to Rabaul by a fleet of small ships that bring in cocoa and timber for export. There are direct shipping services to Europe, Australia, Japan, and the United States.

Rabaul has a large, modern hospital and a fine technical college. In addition, two of the oldest missions have their headquarters in or near Rabaul. There is a large lumber mill and a shipbuilding yard. Commercial firms and banks handling international trade do business here.

Rabaul Public Library (left) and a shopping area (right) in Rabaul

THE INDUSTRIAL CITY OF LAE

The establishment of a cash crop economy has brought about the growth of towns to handle the trade and commerce of the area. At first these urban centers were all ports–Rabaul; Port Moresby; Samarai, just off the eastern tip of the mainland; Kavieng, on New Ireland; and Madang, on the mainland's northern coast, which served the neighboring plantations at Lae. Air transportation extended Madang's link to the mountainous area at its back door, but the building of the Highlands Highway subsequently diverted much of the highland's trade to Lae.

The growth of Lae, in the Huon Gulf, is related to the economic development of the Wau and Bulolo goldfields. When some of the

The area around the city of Lae

dredging around Bulolo ceased, workers found substitute employment at a large plywood mill, which was built in the 1970s. The lumber industry is based on the large stands of hoop and klinkii pines that grow in the mid-mountain valleys.

Lae, now the major industrial city of Papua New Guinea, increased in population 16 percent in two years, from 1969 to 1971. Lae is also a service center for agriculture activities in the area. Since 1971 Lae's population has expanded rapidly, and in 1990 it had more than 80,000 residents.

Growth brought new problems. Energy requirements, sufficient water supply, and sewage disposal facilities had to be addressed. The first study, called the "Lae Project," was conducted by a research team from the Human Ecology Unit of the Australian National University in 1976. For a group of highlanders from Chimbu Province, particular attention was paid to a comparison of living conditions in their rural villages with those in the urban setting to which many of them had migrated.

Homes and gardens in the village of Goroka in the Victor Emanuel Range

Even dietary preferences have changed. The remote villages have felt the effect of the city's market economy. Village stores now stock imported foodstuffs and consumer goods from Lae. In the country there is a certain amount of malnutrition in children because the bulk of their food consists of sweet potatoes. There is also a high incidence of gastrointestinal and respiratory infections due to lack of hygiene, but the incidence of degenerative diseases such as diabetes and heart disease, as well as dental problems, is low. However, in the city where the diet has more variety, foods are higher in fat and sugar content, with a corresponding increase in these degenerative diseases.

Studies of energy use and waste disposal have led to practical measures for conserving energy. One example is the use of sawdust and other residues from a growing lumber industry as useful items for producing compost. A conversion system was commissioned in 1980 to set up a pilot project for the recovery of sewage as sludge, which eventually becomes a liquid fertilizer for use in agriculture. The project also manufactures methane gas for industry and transportation.

Garden plots within the city are allotted to families to grow food. This has relieved indiscriminate gardening on adjacent hills, which had caused devastating erosion. A project has been designed to replant the hillsides to stop soil erosion and to provide future firewood.

One indirect result of the study showed how the position of women in society has been affected. The movement of men from village to city to work as laborers forced the women left behind to fill traditional male roles as well as their own. Women who accompanied their husbands to urban areas were less fortunate. Dependent on the husband's earnings for food, they could no longer use their skills in gardening or caring for farm animals, which had been their routine before. Frequently families separated because of the problems that stemmed from the change to a cash economy, which has undermined the traditional village patterns of power and wealth.

SAVING THE EARTH

A big problem for future development is that Papua New Guineans, like everybody else, are beginning to understand the meaning of saving the earth. They are complaining about dumping toxic waste from the Ok Tedi mine into the Fly River. The cost of building a dam to store the waste on remote mountain tops would make the mines too costly to operate at a profit.

FUTURE PREDICTIONS FOR DEVELOPMENT

Oil is a commodity Papua New Guinea may soon be exporting. All the oil to which access is easy has been found. Now survey crews are combing the countryside on foot, not by plane. They are being led into the interior by local guides who know the terrain as patterns of the landscape passed from one generation to another like folklore. Scientists are "fingerprinting" formations so they are able to connect a bit of one outcrop to a matching second one ten miles (sixteen kilometers) or more away, no matter how geological forces have twisted layers. Drilling crews come in and drill 70 to 150 holes, which are then filled with explosive charges.

The recording crew follows, stringing fiber-optic cables and planting hundreds of geophones, specialized microphones that will record and measure the density of rock strata, revealed by explosion of the charges. The data are then analyzed by geologists at the scientific headquarters at the coastal city of Rumbai. All of this is very time-consuming, and the profit edge is closely watched. If the supply warrants mass development, pipelines will be laid, storage vats constructed, and refineries built. Production of petroleum began in 1992 at about 150,000 barrels per day. In 1994 plans were approved to construct two oil refineries at Port Moresby and Kopi.

A consortium of six companies, headed by Chevron, has found oil in Iagifu-Hedina, in the southern highlands. The decision to develop the field has been delayed because of the expense required to construct a 175-mile (282-kilometer) pipeline and a total development cost of $1 billion. But the question of development seems to be when rather than whether. Once the pipeline is built, it could justify the development of further oil reserves known to exist in the area.

If all the gold mines and oil fields are developed as planned in the next decade, the World Bank forecasts that exports will triple

Data processors (left) employed in an oil company and a chemist (right) working in an insecticide laboratory

by 1997 and that government mineral revenues will more than quadruple. However, the minerals boom will have little direct impact on incomes and jobs of the total population. Mining employs only 0.3 percent of the labor force. The benefit to the bulk of the population will depend on how revenues are channeled into productive investments elsewhere.

THE ECONOMY

While making grandiose claims for capital growth, economic benefits for the person on the street and in the jungle have fallen far behind promises.

There is a shortage of skilled labor, which means that those with little training can demand high wages. The result is that the average wage in the manufacturing industry is three times that of the Philippines, almost twice that of Malaysia, and higher even than that in South Korea. Since productivity is low in Papua New Guinea because of poor training and education, the gap in unit wage costs is wider still. This discourages public investment.

Instead of bringing wages down, the government hopes to lower the cost of manufactured goods by raising the quality and speed of production so that retail prices can compete with the cost of imported goods. In a significant policy change, the government almost doubled the amount it is spending on education.

Another deterrent to industrialization is the country's bad transportation system. The capital, Port Moresby, is still not linked by road to any other large town. Mining roads and old military paths cannot fill the need. Airstrips are being enlarged, but the rugged terrain frequently rules out large aircraft.

One other problem is the increasing scale of more violent crime with guns in larger towns. Many blame the crime on the traditional system of *wantok*, literally "one talk," through which clan members share each other's wealth. The wantok system encourages the young to drift to the towns, knowing that their clansmen will feed and shelter them. In turn, the youths share the spoils of their crimes with their extended families.

If the government can compete in world trade for goods and services and at the same time prune its inefficient bureaucracy, there is a chance that Papua New Guinea will step into the twenty-first century ahead of its neighbors.

BORDER PROBLEMS

In 1984 more than nine thousand refugees crossed into Papua New Guinea from Irian Jaya, the Indonesian half of the island of New Guinea. This sudden migration put a burden on the local economy. For many years relations between Papua New Guinea and Indonesia had been strained because of the military measures taken by the Indonesians against the Melanesian rebels of Irian Jaya who were fighting for independence. This brought about sympathetic concerns from the largely Melanesian population of Papua New Guinea.

Most of the population of Irian Jaya are descendants of early Dutch colonists and Indonesians. However, a group of Melanesians living in the interior feel much closer to their Papua New Guinean neighbors, who share their cultural and ethnic roots. Living in Irian Jaya, they feel like second-class citizens. They tried to set up an independent governing body for Melanesians in Irian Jaya, but were defeated by the Indonesian army.

Over the years many slipped across the border into Papua New Guinea. When the exodus became a growing problem, a 1984 border treaty was signed between Irian Jaya and the government of Papua New Guinea to improve security in the region. Attempts were made to repatriate the refugees with a promise that there would be no reprisals by the Indonesian government against those who returned. But few wanted to return.

In September 1985 the border agreement was reviewed. Prime Minister Somare announced that Papua New Guinea would consider permanent resettlement of genuine refugees. By mid-1986 more than 12,000 refugees were living in camps near the border, and only 760 had taken the opportunity to return home to Irian Jaya without punishment. Several meetings were held between the two governments, but there was still border violence.

In April 1988 two men were killed by Indonesian soldiers, who had crossed into Papua New Guinea in search of rebel leaders. Somare, who was now foreign affairs minister, denounced the action. Soldiers on both sides of the border patrol that area, but no solution has yet been reached on what to do with the increasing number of migrants who want to stay in Papua New Guinea, where democracy is a reality.

PART OF THE WORLD ORDER

In March 1987 talks were held between representatives of the Papua New Guinea and Solomon Islands governments, following reports of violence on Shortland Islands and Choiseul Island, part of the Solomon chain of islands. The inhabitants complained that their waters were being "invaded" by Papua New Guinean fishers. In January 1989 an agreement was reached on a maritime boundary between the two countries.

After the 1987 election, Prime Minister Wingti announced that his government planned to pursue a policy of close diplomatic relations with countries outside the Pacific region. In March 1988 Papua New Guinea signed an agreement with Vanuatu, a group of islands southeast of the Solomons, and the Solomon Islands to form the "Spearhead Group," dedicated to the preservation of Melanesian cultural traditions and to achieving independence for the French Overseas Territory of New Caledonia. In February 1989 it was announced that Papua New Guinea would reduce import tariffs on selected products from Vanuatu and the Solomon Islands in an attempt to stimulate trade between the three countries. Agricultural produce has been the major source of trade.

Papua New Guinea plans to take an active part in creating policies within its sphere of influence—on its own terms and in its own time schedule.

In 1986 the Papua New Guinea Parliament voted to delay the introduction of television into the country. Anyone operating a TV

The Papua New Guinea Bank Corporation in Port Moresby

station could be fined up to a million dollars. "We don't want to be made into Americans or Australians," the minister of education said. "We are proud of our heritage."

However, the Parliament was forced to rescind the order in response to popular demand. In 1993 an estimated ten thousand television sets were able to receive limited programs broadcast from Port Moresby. Shortwave radio supplements telephone service in outlying provinces.

Although Papua New Guineans have vetoed a rush for change, they joined the United Nations in 1975 and have taken an active role in recognizing their integral part in the world order. They cannot hide away in the hills and valleys of their land as they did for hundreds of years.

Papua New Guinea is also a member of the World Bank, the Asian Development Bank (ADB), the Non-Aligned Movement (NAM), and other international organizations. It holds observer status in the Association of South East Asian Nations (ASEAN).

In 1992 Michael Somare, then foreign minister of Papua New Guinea, almost became president of the General Assembly of the United Nations. Somare lost to Saudi Arabia's representative Samir Shihabi by a slim margin of votes. It was reported that the loss had nothing to do with the politics of the countries involved, only their geographic placement. Saudi Arabia is apt to be more involved with Middle Eastern diplomacy and might sway a concession for peace in that area.

Papua New Guinea's time will come; in the meantime, with a new generation of educated citizens, progress in raising living standards is bound to accelerate.

Papua New Guineans plan to follow the words of Michael Somare on the first day of independence. "This is just the beginning. Now we must stand on our own two feet and work harder than ever before."

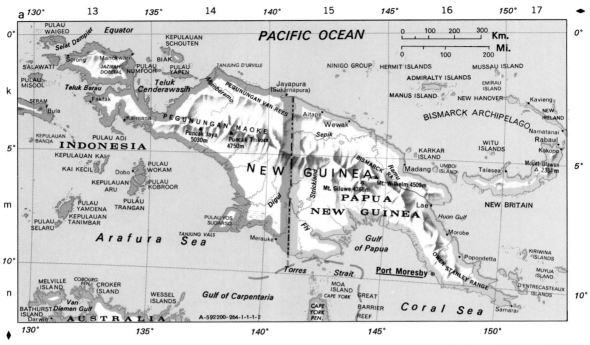

Map from Quick Reference World Atlas
© 1993 by Rand McNally, R.L. 93-S-175

MAP KEY

MINI-FACTS AT A GLANCE

GENERAL INFORMATION

Official Name: Independent State of Papua New Guinea

Capital: Port Moresby

Government: Papua New Guinea is a constitutional monarchy. The British monarch is the chief of state, and is represented locally by a governor-general of native origin. Legislative power rests with the National Parliament of 109 members, elected for five years. The prime minister is the head of the government. The Executive Council appointed by the prime minister is responsible to the Parliament. The judicial system is comprised of the Supreme Court, the National Court, local courts, and village courts. For administrative purposes the country is divided into 20 provinces including one national capital district, Port Moresby.

Religion: Papua New Guinea does not have any official religion. Traditional religious beliefs are still very powerful; belief in magic is widespread. Inanimate objects such as plants, trees, mountains, and rivers are supposed to have miraculous powers. Christianity has gradually replaced the forms of indigenous beliefs. The Missouri Synod of the Lutheran church was one of the first missionary groups to make contact with the indigenous people. Today 58 percent of the population is Protestant, followed by 33 percent Roman Catholic, and 9 percent other religions.

Ethnic Composition: Melanesians are a dark-skinned people with dark woolly and wavy hair, rugged features, and large jaws. Roughly 95 percent of Papua New Guinea's indigenous population belongs to this ethnic group. The Melanesians of Papua New Guinea are descendants of the Ainoids – ancestors of the early Australian aborigines, easily recognized by their heavy brow ridges. Foreigners are from Australia, China, Europe, New Zealand, the Philippines, the United Kingdom, and the United States.

Language: Although English is the official language, a special mixture of languages called Pidgin English is universally spoken. The Melanesian Pidgin has evolved from English, German, and Malay words strung together in largely Melanesian grammar; about 1,500 English words make up approximately 90 percent of Pidgin English's small basic vocabulary. English is spoken by less than 2 percent of the population. There are 715 different indigenous languages or dialects. Motu is spoken in the Papua region.

National Flag: The present design was first used in 1971, but was officially adopted for the flag in 1975. It consists of a rectangle divided diagonally from the upper left corner to the lower right with the upper section in red and lower section in black. A golden bird of paradise appears in the center of the red field; the five white stars of the Southern Cross constellation appear in the black field and identify Papua New Guinea's place under the heavens. Red and black colors are chosen because of their extensive use in native art; the bird of paradise provides feathers for traditional dress and for ceremonies.

National Anthem: "O, Arise All You Sons of This Land"

Money: The Papua New Guinea kina (K) of 100 toea is the official currency. In October 1995 one Papua New Guinea kina was worth approximately $.76 in United States currency.

Membership in International Organizations: Asian Development Bank (ADB); Colombo Plan; Commonwealth of Nations; International Cocoa Organization; International Coffee Organization; International Monetary Fund (IMF); International Natural Rubber Organization; Lome Convention; Non-Aligned Movement (NAM); South Pacific Forum; South Pacific Commission; United Nations (UN); World Bank.

Weights and Measures: The metric system is in force.

Population: 4,443,000 (1996 estimate); 85 percent rural and 15 percent urban; population density 24 persons per sq. mi. (9 persons per sq km)

Cities:

Port Moresby	193,242
Lae	80,655
Madang	27,057
Wewak	23,224
Goroka	17,855

(Population based on 1990 census.)

GEOGRAPHY

Border: The country lies between the equator and 12 degrees south latitude. Its nearest neighbors are Australia to the south, the Federated States of Micronesia to the north, and the Solomon Islands to the east. In the west, it shares a land border of 483 mi. (777 km) with the Irian Jaya province of Indonesia. The coastline is frequently bordered by impenetrable swamps.

Coastline: 2,358 mi. (3,795 km)

Land: Papua New Guinea shares the island of New Guinea, the second largest island in the world, with the province of Irian Jaya of Indonesia. The country includes many islands to the north, east, and south, including islands from the Bismarck Archipelago, New Britain, and the Admiralty Islands. New Britain is the largest of the islands and Bougainville is the most easterly of the larger islands. All larger islands are the tops of a submerged mountain range and most of them are fringed with coral. The New Guinea part of the country makes up about 85 percent of the country's total land. The coast in the southwest forms one of the most extensive swamps in the world. Farther inland, swampy grasslands, reed marshes, and lakes are part of the terrain; sink holes are frequent.

Mountains are the major physical feature. The Victor Emanuel Range rises about 10,000 ft. (3,048 m) from the southwestern coast. The Owen Stanley Mountains stretch in the southern part of the New Guinea Island. A ring of volcanoes is located offshore in two large arcs. Mount Lamington erupted in 1951, killing nearly 3,000 people. Vulcan and Tavurvur erupted in 1994 nearly destroying Rabaul.

Highest Point: Mount Wilhelm, at 14,793 ft. (4,509 m)

Lowest Point: Sea level

Rivers: The Fly, Kikori, Markham, Ramu, Sepik, and Turama are the major rivers. The Fly River is the longest (700 mi.; 1,127 km) and is navigable for 500 mi. (805 km) in all seasons. Most of the rivers are fast-flowing and often torrential.

Forests: Some 85 percent of land is under forests. Vegetation is often very dense, and about 200 different species of trees flourish. Laurel, oak, beech, red cedar, nutmeg, local mahoganies, linkii, and hoop pine trees grow at about 3,000 ft. (914 m). Above 12,000 ft. (3,658 m) the vegetation consists of Alpine grasses, yellow buttercups, and deep blue gentians. Orchids, lilies, ferns, and creepers abound in the lowland rain forests.

Wildlife: Nearly 180 mammals and 70 kinds of bats live in Papua New Guinea. Wildlife includes tree kangaroos, cuscuses, possums, wallabies, bandicoots, pouched "mice," brilliant-colored tree frogs, and echidnas (egg-laying mammals). Some 660 recognized species of birds are found in Papua New Guinea as compared to 500 in North America. The spectacular bird-of-paradise is protected by law. A cassowary is a flightless bird about 3 ft. (0.9 m) tall, hunted almost to extinction. In 1992 a University of Chicago biologist on a field trip in Papua New Guines jungles discovered a poisonous hooded pitohui bird whose skin and feathers were naturally laced with potent neurotoxin.

Many varieties of snakes live in the swampland. Pythons can reach 22 ft. (6.7 m) in length. Huge crocodiles live in the rivers; some spiders are extremely poisonous. Mosquitoes abound everywhere, especially in the swampy areas. Exotic butterflies are raised on several butterfly farms for export to the outside world.

Climate: It is a land of climate extremes. An average of more than 60 in. (152 cm) of rain falls each year; it exceeds over 300 in. (762 cm) in some portions of the south, and over 400 in. (1,016 cm) along the slopes of the main ridges. The temperatures rarely climb above 90° F. (32.2° C), or dip below 70° F. (21.1° C). Frosts are common at 10,000 ft. (3,048 m), and occasional snow falls on Mount Wilhelm. The northwest or wet monsoons blow from December to April and the southeast or dry trade winds blow from May to October. Relative humidity is uniformly high in the lowlands at about 80 percent.

Greatest Distance: North to South, 730 mi. (1,174 km)
East to West, 1,040 mi. (1,674 km)
Area: 178,704 sq mi. (462,840 sq km)

ECONOMY AND INDUSTRY

Agriculture: Roughly less than 1 percent of land is under permanent cultivation, but about three-fifths of the population is engaged in agricultural activity. The slash-and-burn form of agriculture is still very much in use, leaving the soil exhausted and the vegetation destroyed. Some 90 percent of all land is owned by clans under community title and cannot be bought, sold, or leased by individuals. The chief crops are bananas, coconuts, sweet potatoes, sugarcane, taro, yams, cassava, coffee, cocoa, rubber, and pineapples. Yams can be stored for a long time. Coffee accounts for almost 5 percent of export earnings. Rice farming is a recent introduction.

Whales and dolphins abound in the warm waters surrounding the islands. Sea cucumbers are dried and sold in large quantities to Japan and Malaysia; a small green snail also is harvested and exported to Japan. Shark oil is exported in large quantities.

Mining: The Panguna Copper Mine on Bougainville Island is one of the largest of its kind in the world, producing some 2 percent of the world's copper, when operating. The Porgera Gold Mine is the biggest gold mine outside South Africa. Gold and copper account for more than two-thirds of Papua New Guinea's exports. Mineral wealth is paid into the *Mineral Resources Stabilization Fund*, of which only a part is drawn by the government for spending each year. Chevron has found oil in the southern highlands near Lake Kutubu. The Kutubu Project started producing oil in 1992. Studies have also confirmed large natural gas reserves, and a two-train liquified natural gas facility is in the planning stages. Other minerals found are chromite, cobalt, nickel, quartz, and silver.

Manufacturing: Manufacturing is limited to food products, beverages, tobacco, wood products, metal products, and small machinery and transport equipment. A shipbuilding yard and a lumber mill are at Rabaul; a large plywood factory operates at Lae, the major industrial city of Papua New Guinea. Energy is largely derived from hydroelectric power.

Transportation: The transport infrastructure is not yet developed in the country. There are no railroads; total road length is about 12,300 mi. (19,840 km), out of which 398 miles (627 kilometers) are paved. The Highlands Highway connects some remote areas in the central highlands. Main international airport is at Port Moresby; there are some 400 other smaller airports and airstrips throughout the country. The government-owned *Air Niugini* is the national airline; *Talair Phy* is a smaller airline with service to some 130 destinations in Papua New Guinea. Rabaul is the country's main port for exports; a fleet of small ships brings in cocoa and timber to Rabaul for export. There are some 15 other ports and a coastal fleet of about 300 vessels.

Communication: There are two English daily newspapers, *The Papua New Guinea Post-Courier* and *The National*. Television sets in remote areas are able to receive limited programs broadcast from Port Moresby. Outlying provinces have shortwave radio service and telephone facilities. Radio broadcasts are made in English, Pidgin, Motu, and a dozen other languages. In the early 1990s there was one radio receiver per 16 persons, one television set per 350 persons, and one telephone per 50 persons.

Trade: The chief imports are machinery and transport equipment, mineral fuels, lubricants, food, consumer goods, and chemicals. Major import sources are Australia, Japan, the United States, Singapore, New Zealand, the United Kingdom, China, and Germany. Chief export items are copper ore, gold, coffee, timber, cocoa beans, palm oil, and copra. Major export destinations are Japan, Germany, Australia, South Korea, the United Kingdom, and the United States. In the early 1990s, Papua New Guinea had a trade surplus.

EVERYDAY LIFE

Health: Life expectancy at 56 years for males and 57 years for females is low. Major illnesses are pneumonia, malaria, typhoid, measles, whooping cough, diarrhea, dysentery, leprosy, skin infections, meningitis, and tuberculosis. Less than one-third of the population has access to safe drinking water. The government is trying to establish health services throughout the country, especially in the remote areas, and is spending about 11 percent of its budget on social and health services. Several Christian missions also provide health and medical services. Rabaul has a large modern hospital. In the early 1990s there were about 12,000 people per physician, and some 220 persons per hospital bed. Infant mortality rate at 53 per 1,000 live births is high. (In the US the infant mortality rate is 8 per 1,000.)

Education: Six years of education are compulsory and free. Primary education begins at seven years of age and lasts for six years. Secondary education begins at the age of 13 and lasts for six years. The curricula has been designed to permit students to return to work in the rural areas, where most of the population still lives. Advanced education is provided by the University of Papua New Guinea at Port Moresby and the University of Technology at Lae. There are a few teacher training colleges and other vocational institutions. In 1995 the literacy rate was about 52 percent.

Holidays:

January 1, New Year's Day
July 23, Remembrance Day
August 15, National Constitution Day
September 16, Independence Day
December 25, Christmas

Movable holidays include Good Friday, Easter Monday, and the Queen's Birthday.

Culture: The Sepik people display one of the richest forms of primitive art in the world; spirit masks, shields, canoe prows, musical instruments, bowls, and even cooking pots are lavishly decorated. The Motuans, who live around Port Moresby, make excellent clay cooking pots. Devon women make baskets of all sizes; they also make strings from the barks of hibiscus plants that in turn are used to make fringed skirts. Men make sculptures in wood sometimes decorated with shells or crocodile teeth. There are some 25 libraries, but the two major libraries exist with the universities. The Papua New Guinea National Museum and Art Gallery are at Port Moresby.

Society: Bonds of kinship are recognized and social obligations extend beyond the immediate family group. There is a strong attachment of the people to the land. Dobu Islanders have a matriarchal society; children inherit their mother's and maternal uncle's land and property. In rural areas a groom must present golden-edge clamshells as the bride price. Some people scar their skin in bold patterns.

Bougainville people are efficient farmers; they cultivate large gardens and raise pigs and taro, a root crop. They trade pigs for shell money, which is in turn used as currency.

Dress: Special ceremonies are marked by wearing elaborate bird-of-paradise plumed headpieces by men. Bones or wooden barbs are pierced through their nostrils and colored clay is patterned on their bodies. Women wear cowrie shell necklaces and mother-of-pearl plates as a sign of wealth and status.

Housing: Rural houses are built with the simplest tools and materials. The broad-leaved sago palm fronds are used for thatching roofs, and the trunks are used for building fences and houses. The Sepik people live in large villages. The dwellings are built on stilts to protect against flooding. Large rows of houses are built in parallel lines facing a cleared space of ground where dances and ceremonial festivals are held. There is an acute shortage of housing in the urban areas because of mass migration. The government has built low-cost housing in Port Moresby and Lae.

Food: Papua New Guinea food consists of yams, sweet potatoes, taro, manioc, bananas, and sago. Coconut appears with almost every meal. There is very little meat in the daily diet. Birds and crocodiles are hunted for food. Rivers provide a great variety of edible fish as well as prawns, crocodiles, turtles, crayfish, crabs, lobsters, and other shellfish. The national drink is *kava*, made from the root of a pepper plant. Chewing betel nut is a habit of the Nogullos people. Bougainville people eat roasted or steamed pork, boiled eel and opossum, vegetables, and nut puddings at village celebrations.

Sports and Recreation: Water sports, golf, tennis, rock-climbing, spear throwing, archery, tracking small game, and hunting are popular pastimes.

Sing-sings are organized as celebrations for a variety of events. Dancing and chanting to a rhythmic beat are popular. For dances men and women transform themselves into trees, birds, animals, or mountain spirits; loud chants are accompanied by banging hollow tubes together; leather-covered drums are beaten. Some gatherings last for two or three days.

Social Welfare: There is no organized social welfare system in Papua New Guinea. However, a certain amount of the national budget is set aside for health and social relief work in urban areas. Some Christian missionaries provide relief work with government assistance to the needy. In general, families tend to take care of their own.

IMPORTANT DATES

1365—The land of New Guinea is mentioned in Javanese literature

1545—Name "New Guinea" is given to the island by Spaniard Ynigo Ortis de Retes

1569—*Nueva Guinea* appears for the first time on the world map

1793—Attempts are made by the British to set up a trading center for spices on New Guinea

1828—The Dutch take possession of the southwest coast of New Guinea

1835—The Dutch Fort Merkusoord is abandoned

1846—The British take possession of the New Guinea coast

1864—A severe earthquake and tidal wave destroy the Christian missionary complex on the island of Mansinam

1871—The London Mission Society installs teachers on the islands in the Torres Strait area

1873—Captain Moresby discovers the site where the town of Port Moresby later developed

1874—The London Missionary Society establishes a mission near Port Moresby

1884—Polynesian pastors arrive in the Gulf of Papua; the first native pastors are graduated from the London Missionary Society; Germans claim northeastern New Guinea along with the Bismarck Archipelago, and set up a temporary trading post

1885—An agreement between the Dutch and the British divides the island of New Guinea

1888—Gold is discovered in New Guinea; Britain annexes the territory as the crown colony of British New Guinea

1899—German New Guinea is made an imperial colony administered by German government officials

1901—Australia becomes independent of Great Britain

1902—British New Guinea passes to Australia

1906—Australian rule is established over the Territory of Papua

1918—Germany surrenders, ending the First World War, which began in 1914

1921—The former German New Guinea is placed under a League of Nations mandate administered by Australia

1921-22—The Kremer Expedition discovers the Grand Valley

1926—A gold rush begins in the Edie Creek and the Bulolo River area

1930—A Stone-Age civilization of about one million people is discovered in the highlands

1939-45—World War II

1940—The last *hiri,* or trading voyage, takes place

1942—The Japanese reach the island of New Britain

1945—Australia appoints a chief administrator for both Papua and New Guinea territories

1949—Australia establishes a joint administration of the Territories of Papua and the Trust Territory of New Guinea; the union is named the Territory of Papua and New Guinea

1951—Mount Lamington erupts; a Legislative Council is established for the Territory of Papua and New Guinea

1964—The Legislative Council is replaced by a House of Assembly

1971—The territory is renamed as Papua New Guinea

1972—Panguna Copper mine is opened

1975—Papua New Guinea gains independence; the House of Assembly becomes the National Parliament; the independent country joins the United Nations; the kina is introduced as the national currency; Michael Somare becomes the first prime minister

1976—The Human Ecology Unit of the Australian National University conducts a research study for the economic development of the town of Lae

1977—The nation's first general elections are held

1978—Provincial governments are established in all 20 provinces; a widespread tribal riot takes place

1980—A conversion system is commissioned to convert raw sewage into liquid fertilizer and methane gas to be used in industry and transportation

1982—Somare is reelected as prime minister

1984—More than 9,000 refugees cross the border from Irian Jaya, Indonesia, to Papua New Guinea; a border treaty is signed between these two nations

1985—Prime Minister Somare survives a no-confidence vote; he reviews the border treaty

1986—Parliament votes to delay the introduction of television to the country

1987—General elections take place; talks are held between Papua New Guinea and Solomon Island governments

1988—Free primary education is introduced; Papua New Guinea, Solomon Islands, and Vanuatu sign an agreement to form the "Melanesian Spearhead Group" to preserve the Melanesian culture; French marine naturalist Jacques Cousteau films a record number of sea creatures for almost a year; two Papuan citizens are killed by Indonesian soldiers at the border

1989—The Panguna Copper mine is closed; an agreement is reached on a maritime boundary between the Solomon Islands and Papua New Guinea

1991—The airstrip at Hewa is completed; the Pactra II agreement with Australia establishes a free trade zone and protects Australian investments in Papua New Guinea

1992—Michael Somare loses the bid to become president of the General Assembly of the United Nations by a slim margin of votes; a 162-mi. (261-km) long marine and land pipeline is completed from Kutubu oilfields to a petroleum export platform in the Gulf of New Guinea

1993—Parliament allows the introduction of television in the country; Papua New Guinea signs an agreement with Russia and Australia for the establishment of a 'spaceport' in the New Ireland Province that will launch commercial rockets by the late 1990s

1994—Sir Julius Chan is elected prime minister; Chan negotiates peace terms with Sam Kavona, leader of the Revolutionary Army, about the Bougainville area with a peace conference to follow; more than 100,000 are forced to flee their homes in Rabaul as the Vulcan and Tavurvur volcanoes erupt and nearly destroy the city in the country's worst recorded natural disaster

1995—A proposal by the former prime minister Wingti to abolish the provincial government system is rejected by the Chan government; widespread rioting takes place during provincial elections in the Western Highlands Province

1996—In accordance with the report from the Papua New Guinea National Research Institute that forest resources are depleting quickly, the government decides to reduce timber export by 10 percent

IMPORTANT PEOPLE

Josephine Abaijah, the only woman in the 109-member Papua New Guinea Parliament; leader of a separatist movement of the southern region

Otto Eduard Leopold von Bismarck (1815-98), German Chancellor; also called the Iron Chancellor; ruled during time of German settlement in New Guinea

Sir Julius Chan, leader of the People's Progressive Party; prime minister 1980-82 and in 1994

Jacques-Yves Cousteau (1910-   ), noted French naval officer, ocean explorer, and naturalist; spent about a year with his crew filming a number of unknown sea creatures in Papua New Guinea in 1988

Queen Elizabeth II (1926-   ), British queen since 1953, constitutional head of Papua New Guinea and Commonwealth of Nations

Vincent Eri, author; major publication is *The Crocodile*

Sir John Guise, elected governor-general in 1977

Captain John Hayes, British naval officer; he declared the island possession of Great Britain and built Fort Coronation in 1793

Sir Albert Maori Kiki, (1931-   ), author; major publication is *Kiki: Ten Thousand Years in a Lifetime*

Sir Wiwa Korowi, (1948-   ), governor-general since November 1991

Michael and Dan Leahy, two Australians who discovered a Stone Age civilization in the New Guinea highlands on May 27, 1930; they filmed and recorded their meetings with these "new" people

Sir George LuHunte, the second British lieutenant-governor in the late 1890s

Sir William MacGregor, named the first British lieutenant-governor in 1888; he mapped the coastlines and navigable rivers

Captain John McCluer, a British naval officer, arrived in New Guinea in 1794

Don Jorge de Meneses, Portuguese governor of Maluka; landed on the island of New Guinea in 1526; the first white man to set foot on the island; he called the island for the first time "Papua"

Captain John Moresby, claimed eastern part of New Guinea for Britain in 1873; Port Moresby is named after him

Hubert Murray, the first Australian lieutenant-governor of the Territory of Papua, 1908-40

Rabbie Namaliu (1947-   ), fourth prime minister, 1988-92; the first prime minister to hold a university degree (1970); leader of Pangu Pati (Papua New Guinea United party)

Francis Ona, a rebel leader from Bougainville

Ynigo Ortiz de Retes, named the island *Nueva Guinea* in 1545

Vice Admiral Freiherr G. von Schleinitz, German official who explored the Sepik River for 200 mi. (322 km) in 1872

Dr. Charles Schraeder, German naturalist who explored the Sepik River in late 1800s

Michael Thomas Somare (1936-   ), first prime minister of independent Papua New Guinea (1975-80); also served as the chief minister in an interim coalition government, 1972-75; served as prime minister again 1982-86; also minister of foreign affairs (until 1993); and the country's representative to the United Nations

Captain Owen Stanley, British officer who explored the coasts of New Guinea from 1845 to 1850; the Owen Stanley Range is named after him

Luiz Vaez de Torres (early 1600s), Spaniard who visited Mainu island in 1606

Gough Whitlam, Australian prime minister in the mid-1970s

Paias Wingti (1951-   ), leader of the People's Democratic Movement (PDM); elected as prime minister in 1985, 1988, 1992, and 1994

Compiled by Chandrika Kaul, Ph.D.

INDEX
Page numbers that appear in boldface type indicate illustrations

About the Author

Mary Virginia Fox was graduated from Northwestern University in Evanston, Illinois, and now lives near Madison, Wisconsin, across the lake from the state capitol and the University of Wisconsin. She is the author of more than two dozen books for young adults and has had a number of articles published in adult publications.

Mrs. Fox and her husband have lived overseas for several months at a time and enjoy traveling. She considers herself a professional writer and an amateur artist. She has also written *Bahrain, Tunisia, New Zealand, Cyprus,* and *Iran* in the Enchantment of the World series.

SLADE MEDIA CENTER